30
DAYS

By the same author:
Why Jesus?
Why Christmas?
Alpha—Questions of Life
Searching Issues
A Life Worth Living
How to Run the Alpha Course: Telling Others
Challenging Lifestyle
The Heart of Revival

30 DAYS

A Practical Introduction to
Reading the Bible

NICKY GUMBEL

Alpha

Alpha Resources
Alpha North America

Published in North America by Alpha North America, 2275 Half Day Road, Suite 185, Deerfield, IL 60015

© 1999 by Nicky Gumbel

This edition issued by special arrangement with Alpha International, Holy Trinity Brompton, Brompton Road, London SW7 1JA, UK

30 Days
by Nicky Gumbel

Originally published by KINGSWAY COMMUNICATIONS LTD, Lottbridge Drove, Eastbourne, BN23 6NT, England

First printed by Alpha North America in 2003

Printed in the United States of America

Scripture in this publication is from the Holy Bible, New International Version (NIV), Copyright 1973, 1978, 1984 International Bible Society, used by permission of Zondervan. All rights reserved.

Illustrations by Charlie Mackesy

ISBN 978-1-938328-20-6

1 2 3 4 5 6 7 8 9 10 Printing/Year 15 14 13 12

Contents

How to Use This Book

The Bible is the most powerful book that has ever been written. It is a collection of 66 books, written in three languages, and covering more than 1,000 years. Although it was written by human beings over many years, God inspired it and speaks through it today. Studying the Bible not only illuminates our minds; it warms our hearts, feeds our souls, and changes our lives.

The Bible often looks daunting and it is difficult to know where to start. The purpose of *30 Days* is to help those who want to start reading the Bible. There are many ways to go about this. I have selected 30 passages which I have found particularly helpful. Some of the passages are from the Old Testament (which Jesus read and knew well), others are from the Gospels (which concern His life, teaching, death, and resurrection) and the remainder are from the rest of the New Testament (mainly letters written by those close to Jesus).

To get the most out of this book:

- Put aside time each day to be alone with God. A good way to begin is to pray as the Old Testament prophet Samuel prayed: "Speak LORD, for your servant is listening" (1 Samuel 3:9).

- Read and think about the passage from the Bible for the day. Try and sense what God could be saying to you through the passage. Then read the comments that go with it, referring back to the passage as you go along. (The numbers in parentheses refer to the chapter and verse numbers in the Bible.) After God has spoken to you through His word, then speak to Him in prayer.

I find the following a great help in structuring my prayers. The order is easy to remember as the first letter of each section forms the word **ACTS.**

A   Adoration
        – praising God for who He is and what He has done.

C   Confession
        – asking God's forgiveness for anything that we have
            done wrong.

T   Thanksgiving
        – for health, family, friends, and so on.

S   Supplication
        – praying for ourselves, for our friends, and for others.

Getting to know God is the purpose for which we were made. In order to do this we need to spend time speaking to Him and letting Him speak to us. Jesus Himself set for us a great example. Time alone with God has been the key for all the great men and women of God. From Moses to Mother Teresa, from the apostle Paul to Billy Graham. As the prophet wrote,

"He wakens me morning by morning, wakens my ear to listen like one being taught." (Isaiah 50:4b)

God has given us the extraordinary privilege of knowing Him. I hope that by the end of *30 Days* you will want to make spending time with God— speaking to Him and letting Him speak to you—a lifetime habit.

30 DAYS

Bible Passage
Matthew 28:1-10

The Guard at the Tomb

[62]The next day, the one after Preparation Day, the chief priests and the Pharisees went to Pilate. [63]"Sir," they said, "we remember that while he was still alive that deceiver said, 'After three days I will rise again.' [64]So give the order for the tomb to be made secure until the third day. Otherwise, his disciples may come and steal the body and tell the people that he has been raised from the dead. This last deception will be worse than the first."

[65]"Take a guard," Pilate answered. "Go, make the tomb as secure as you know how." [66]So they went and made the tomb secure by putting a seal on the stone and posting the guard.

The Resurrection

28 **After the Sabbath, at dawn on the first day of the week, Mary Magdalene and the other Mary went to look at the tomb.**

[2]There was a violent earthquake, for an angel of the Lord came down from heaven and, going to the tomb, rolled back the stone and sat on it. [3]His appearance was like lightning, and his clothes were white as snow. [4]The guards were so afraid of him that they shook and became like dead men.

[5]The angel said to the women, "Do not be afraid, for I know that you are looking for Jesus, who was crucified. [6]He is not here; he has risen, just as he said. Come and see the place where he lay. [7]Then go quickly and tell his disciples: 'He has risen from the dead and is going ahead of you into Galilee. There you will see him.' Now I have told you."

[8]So the women hurried away from the tomb, afraid yet filled with joy, and ran to tell his disciples. [9]Suddenly Jesus met them. "Greetings," he said. They came to him, clasped his feet and worshiped him. [10]Then Jesus said to them, "Do not be afraid. Go and tell my brothers to go to Galilee; there they will see me."

The Guards' Report

[11]While the women were on their way, some of the guards went into the city and reported to the chief priests everything that had happened. [12]When the chief priests had met with the elders and devised a plan, they gave the soldiers a large sum of money, [13]telling them, "You are to say, 'His disciples came during the night and stole him away while we were asleep.' [14]If this report gets to the governor, we will satisfy him and keep you out of trouble." [15]So the soldiers took the money and did as they were instructed. And this story has been widely circulated among the Jews to this very day.

The Great Commission

[16]Then the eleven disciples went to Galilee, to the mountain where Jesus had told them to go. [17]When they saw him, they worshiped him; but some doubted. [18]Then Jesus came to them and said, "All authority in heaven and on earth has been given to me. [19]Therefore go and make disciples of all nations, baptizing them in the name of the Father and of the Son and of the Holy Spirit, [20]and teaching them to obey everything I have commanded you. And surely I am with you always, to the very end of the age."

The verses to be studied each day are highlighted within their biblical context.

The Most Important Question

If you could meet any person from the past and ask just one question, who would you meet and what would you ask? When he was asked this, Professor C. E. M. Joad, then Professor of Philosophy at London University and a well-known agnostic, answered: "I would meet Jesus Christ and ask Him the most important question in all the world—did You or did You not rise from the dead?"

Either Jesus is alive now and we can know Him or He is not and we cannot. What is the evidence that Jesus is alive?

1. The absence of Jesus from the tomb

When Mary Magdalene and the other Mary went to look at the tomb they found the tombstone rolled away. They were told to go and "see the place where he lay" (vs. 6) so that they could witness the fact that He was no longer there.

"Now Mary, have you looked properly?"

Women were not allowed to be witnesses in court in those days. If Jesus' resurrection had been a hoax and invented by the early Christians, they would never have chosen women to be the first witnesses, so the fact that Matthew records the women's role gives the account an authentic ring.

2. The presence of Jesus with the disciples

These women actually saw Jesus. They met Him (vs. 9) and He spoke to them. They "clasped his feet and worshiped him" (vs. 9). Later on, many others saw Jesus (Matthew 28:16-20; Luke 24:36–51; John 21; 1 Corinthians 15:1-8). More than 500 people saw him on 11 different occasions over a period of six weeks.

3. The birth and growth of the Christian church

These women were utterly changed. They must have been devastated by Jesus' death but that morning they were "filled with joy" (vs. 8). They rushed off to spread the good news (vs. 10). Nothing other than the physical resurrection of Jesus can explain the utter transformation of Mary Magdalene and the other Mary, and then of the disciples, which resulted in the explosive growth of the church.

4. The experience of Christians through the ages

These two women were the first to experience an encounter with the risen Jesus Christ. Since that day countless millions of Christians have had the same experience. C. S. Lewis wrote, "A Christian believes in Jesus not because he finds Him by laboratory methods, but by actual contact with Him. A Christian is something like the electric eel, which knows more about electricity than all the electrical engineers put together."

It was on the basis of all this evidence that Professor Joad came to faith in Jesus Christ in the last years of his life. His final book in which he outlined his new-found faith was called *Recovery of Belief.*

The implications of the resurrection are far-reaching. Dwell on these three extraordinary facts.

You can be sure about the past

God raised Jesus from the dead. You can therefore be sure that the cross was effective and forgiveness is possible.

You can be sure about the future

You can be sure that if you have put your faith in Christ one day you too will rise from the dead just as He did. Death is a defeated tyrant. There is nothing that can ultimately harm us.

You can be sure about the present

You can be sure that Jesus is alive today. He is near you right now. You can hear this same person speak to you (primarily through the Bible) and you can speak to Him (as you pray).

Prayer:

You might like to thank God today for the resurrection of Jesus. Thank Him that it is possible to have the assurance and forgiveness, a secure future, and the presence of Jesus with you each day.

[19]Jesus gave them this answer: "I tell you the truth, the Son can do nothing by himself; he can do only what he sees his Father doing, because whatever the Father does the Son also does. [20]For the Father loves the Son and shows him all he does. Yes, to your amazement he will show him even greater things than these. [21]For just as the Father raises the dead and gives them life, even so the Son gives life to whom he is pleased to give it. [22]Moreover, the Father judges no one, but has entrusted all judgment to the Son, [23]that all may honor the Son just as they honor the Father. He who does not honor the Son does not honor the Father, who sent him.

[24]"I tell you the truth, whoever hears my word and believes him who sent me has eternal life and will not be condemned; he has crossed over from death to life. [25]I tell you the truth, a time is coming and has now come when the dead will hear the voice of the Son of God and those who hear will live. [26]For as the Father has life in himself, so he has granted the Son to have life in himself. [27]And he has given him authority to judge because he is the Son of Man.

[28]"Do not be amazed at this, for a time is coming when all who are in their graves will hear his voice [29]and come out —those who have done good will rise to live, and those who have done evil will rise to be condemned. [30]By myself I can do nothing; I judge only as I hear, and my judgment is just, for I seek not to please myself but him who sent me.

Testimonies About Jesus

[31]"If I testify about myself, my testimony is not valid. [32]There is another who testifies in my favor, and I know that his testimony about me is valid.

[33]"You have sent to John and he has testified to the truth. [34]Not that I accept human testimony; but I mention it that you may be saved. [35]John was a lamp that burned and gave light, and you chose for a time to enjoy his light.

[36]"I have testimony weightier than that of John. For the very work that the Father has given me to finish, and which I am doing, testifies that the Father has sent me. [37]And the Father who sent me has himself testified concerning me. You have never heard his voice nor seen his form, [38]nor does his word dwell in you, for you do not believe the one he sent. [39]You diligently study the Scriptures because you think that by them you possess eternal life. These are the Scriptures that testify about me, [40]yet you refuse to come to me to have life.

[41]"I do not accept praise from men, [42]but I know you. I know that you do not have the love of God in your hearts. [43]I have come in my Father's name, and you do not accept me; but if someone else comes in his own name, you will accept him. [44]How can you believe if you accept praise from one another, yet make no effort to obtain the praise that comes from the only God?

[45]"But do not think I will accuse you before the Father. Your accuser is Moses, on whom your hopes are set. [46]If you believed Moses, you would believe me, for he wrote about me. [47]But since you do not believe what he wrote, how are you going to believe what I say?"

Jesus Feeds the Five Thousand

6 Some time after this, Jesus crossed to the far shore of the Sea of Galilee (that is, the Sea of Tiberias), [2]and a great crowd of people followed him because they saw the miraculous signs he had performed on the sick. [3]Then Jesus went up on a mountainside and sat down with his disciples. [4]The Jewish Passover Feast was near.

[5]When Jesus looked up and saw a great crowd coming toward him, he said to Philip, "Where shall we buy bread for these people to eat?" [6]He asked this only to test him, for he already had in mind what he was going to do.

[7]Philip answered him, "Eight months' wages would not buy enough bread for each one to have a bite!"

Evidence That Demands a Verdict

How do we know that Christianity is true? Jesus made some astonish-ing claims: earlier in this chapter in verse 18, "he was even calling God his own Father, making himself equal with God." But Jesus says His own testimony is not enough (vs. 31). Supporting evidence is required. God the Father has supplied this evidence (vs. 32) through at least four witnesses.

1. The evidence of other people (vs. 33)

John the Baptist had provided supporting evidence. Earlier in the Gospel John tells us that "there came a man who was sent from God; his name was John. He came as a witness to testify concerning that light. . . . He himself was not the light; he came only as a witness to the light" (John 1:6-8).

Today there are millions of Christians all over the world, more than ever before, pointing to Jesus Christ. They come from every race, class, color, and background. They say that Jesus has changed their lives. He is the "Lamb of God, who takes away the sin of the world" (John 1:29).

2. The evidence of the life's work of Jesus (vs. 36)

Jesus says that "the very work that the Father has given me to finish, and which I am doing, testifies that the Father has sent me" (vs. 36). This evidence Jesus describes as "weightier than that of John" (vs. 36). Jesus is, as former Archbishop of Canterbury, William Temple, put it, referring to "the whole activity of the word made flesh." Jesus' life's work includes His miracles, which were openly acknowledged to have happened at the time although some simply attributed them to demonic powers. The evidence also includes His way of life, His attitude to other people, the effect of His teaching, His influence on those who met Him, and supremely His death. Jesus said the purpose for which He was sent by the Father was to die for us (vs. 36). When it was completed, He cried out, "It is finished" (John 19:30).

3. The evidence of the Father's direct testimony (vss. 37-38)

First, there was the outward voice that testified directly at Jesus' baptism, declaring "You are my Son, whom I love" (Mark 1:11). Secondly, there are the inner words of the Father, who speaks to our hearts and consciences (John 15:26). Thirdly, the main way in the New Testament that the Father directly testifies is by raising His Son from the dead (see Acts 2:24).

4. The evidence of the Scriptures (vss. 38-39)

Jesus says, "The Scriptures . . . testify about me" (vs. 39). The whole Old Testament reflects Jesus—"Moses . . . wrote about me" (vs. 46). As the reformer Martin Luther put it: "every word rings of Christ." There are more than 300 prophecies about Him including the virgin birth, the place of His birth, the manner of His death (in great detail), and the place of His burial.

It is possible to read the Bible and miss the whole point. Some of the Jewish people of that day did that. They diligently studied the Scriptures (vs. 39), but life was not to be found in the book. The book is the witness that points to Jesus. Life is in Jesus. As someone has put it, "What is in the old [Testament] concealed is in the new [Testament] revealed."

In the light of all this evidence, why do people refuse to come to Jesus Christ?

Some are not willing to put God first in their lives (vs. 42)

They are not willing to obey the first command (to love God above everything) to give up everything that they know is wrong in their lives.

Some are more concerned about what others think than about what God thinks (vs. 44)

There may be a stigma attached to being known as a Christian and associated with other Christians, but Jesus died publicly for us and we should not be ashamed to be known publicly as His followers.

Some simply refuse to believe in Jesus in spite of the evidence (vss. 40, 47)

We should not be surprised if this is still the case today. It is not belief in Jesus that is irrational but unbelief. It is irrational not to believe in the face of overwhelming evidence.

Prayer:

You could thank God that He has not left us without evidence and that our faith is based on good historical grounds. You could thank Him for the life, death, and resurrection of Jesus Christ.

Bible Passage
Luke 9:18-27

Jesus Feeds the Five Thousand

[10]When the apostles returned, they reported to Jesus what they had done. Then he took them with him and they withdrew by themselves to a town called Bethsaida, [11]but the crowds learned about it and followed him. He welcomed them and spoke to them about the kingdom of God, and healed those who needed healing.

[12]Late in the afternoon the Twelve came to him and said, "Send the crowd away so they can go to the surrounding villages and countryside and find food and lodging, because we are in a remote place here."

[13]He replied, "You give them something to eat."

They answered, "We have only five loaves of bread and two fish —unless we go and buy food for all this crowd." [14](About five thousand men were there.) But he said to his disciples, "Have them sit down in groups of about fifty each." [15]The disciples did so, and everybody sat down. [16]Taking the five loaves and the two fish and looking up to heaven, he gave thanks and broke them. Then he gave them to the disciples to set before the people. [17]They all ate and were satisfied, and the disciples picked up twelve basketfuls of broken pieces that were left over.

Peter's Confession of Christ

[18]Once when Jesus was praying in private and his disciples were with him, he asked them, "Who do the crowds say I am?"

[19]They replied, "Some say John the Baptist; others say Elijah; and still others, that one of the prophets of long ago has come back to life."

[20]"But what about you?" he asked. "Who do you say I am?"

Peter answered, "The Christ of God."

[21]Jesus strictly warned them not to tell this to anyone. [22]And he said, "The Son of Man must suffer many things and be rejected by the elders, chief priests and teachers of the law, and he must be killed and on the third day be raised to life."

[23]Then he said to them all: "If anyone would come after me, he must deny himself and take up his cross daily and follow me. [24]For whoever wants to save his life will lose it, but whoever loses his life for me will save it. [25]What good is it for a man to gain the whole world, and yet lose or forfeit his very self? [26]If anyone is ashamed of me and my words, the Son of Man will be ashamed of him when he comes in his glory and in the glory of the Father and of the holy angels. [27]I tell you the truth, some who are standing here will not taste death before they see the kingdom of God."

The Transfiguration

[28]About eight days after Jesus said this, he took Peter, John and James with him and went up onto a mountain to pray. [29]As he was praying, the appearance of his face changed, and his clothes became as bright as a flash of lightning. [30]Two men, Moses and Elijah, [31]appeared in glorious splendor, talking with Jesus. They spoke about his departure, which he was about to bring to fulfillment at Jerusalem. [32]Peter and his companions were very sleepy, but when they became fully awake, they saw his glory and the two men standing with him. [33]As the men were leaving Jesus, Peter said to him, "Master, it is good for us to be here. Let us put up three shelters—one for you, one for Moses and one for Elijah." (He did not know what he was saying.)

[34]While he was speaking, a cloud appeared and enveloped them, and they were afraid as they entered the cloud. [35]A voice came from the cloud, saying, "This is my Son, whom I have chosen; listen to him."

Is Christianity a Crutch?

At Buchenwald, a concentration camp, 65,000 people were put to death by a totalitarian regime which saw the Christian faith as a threat to the ideology of death. "At Buchenwald there was one block of cells reserved for especially 'dangerous' prisoners. In Cell 27 they placed Paul Schneider, a Lutheran pastor, who came to be called 'the Preacher of Buchenwald.' From the small window in his cell he loudly proclaimed Jesus Christ in defiance of the orders of the Gestapo guards. In Cell 23 they placed Otto Neururer, a Catholic priest, whose work on behalf of the Jews and other so-called undesirables had made him a threat to the Nazi warlords. He, too, ministered to the prisoners in Jesus' name.

"Together, a son of Rome and a son of the Reformation, separated no longer by four centuries but only by four cells, walked the way of the cross and together bore witness to their Lord." (Timothy George, Christianity Today, *June 15, 1998, p.44.)*

Some people say that Christianity is a crutch. A crutch is an artificial support, which is only needed if a part of our body is not functioning correctly. In general, people don't need crutches, although they may make life easier in the short term. People using crutches are anxious to get rid of them as soon as possible. Is Christianity like that?

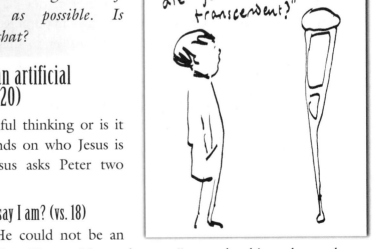

1. Is Christianity an artificial support? (vss. 18-20)

Is it just wishful thinking or is it true? That depends on who Jesus is (vss. 18-20). Jesus asks Peter two questions:

Who do the crowds say I am? (vs. 18)

They knew He could not be an ordinary man. When He was 12 people were "amazed at his understanding and his answers" (Luke 2:47). When they heard His first talk the "eyes of everyone . . . were fastened on him" (Luke 4:20). They had seen Him heal lepers and those who were paralyzed.

They had heard His teaching. They had even seen Him raise someone from the dead (Luke 7:11-17), and therefore thought He must be the reincarnation of someone great. People are still speculating today about who Jesus might be. But Jesus asks another question.

Who do you say I am? (vs. 20)

We cannot rely on second-hand opinions. Each one of us has to make our own decision based on the available evidence. Peter's reply is "The Christ of God." He was absolutely right. Jesus is the Christ, the Son of God. There is good historical evidence for this in the life, death, and resurrection of Jesus Christ. There is good reason to believe. This is not wishful thinking. It is not a crutch. It is not artificial. This is reality.

2. Is it only for especially weak or needy people? (vss. 21-23)

Jesus said, "The Son of Man must suffer." The Greek word for "must" means "necessary for certain great ends." Jesus came, died, and rose again because He loves us. He came "for certain great ends"—to meet universal needs. We have physical needs such as food, water, and air. We can only survive about three months without food, three days without water and three minutes without air. Yet are food, water, and air "crutches"? No; they are universal physical needs.

All human beings, whether they know it or not, have emotional and spiritual needs. We have a need for meaning and purpose, for hope beyond death, and for an answer to guilt. The answer to these needs is not a crutch. It is the cross and resurrection of Jesus Christ.

3. Is it something which makes life easier? (vss. 23-26)

Is Christianity an escape? Is it a quick fix like drugs? Jesus' words make it quite clear that it is not easy, although it is exciting and challenging. It is not easy for three reasons:

No sin

Jesus says that those who follow Him must "deny themselves" (vs. 23). We need to give up what we know to be wrong. We cannot hang on to sin. That would be the easy way out.

No self

Jesus says we must take up our cross daily (vs. 23). Anyone who had watched a crucifixion would know that this was no easy option. It means a daily dying to our own selfishness.

No secrecy

Jesus calls us to follow Him (vs. 26). He was asking people to declare their faith in Him publicly. We cannot be secret disciples. Jesus wants His followers to stand up and be counted, even when it is difficult to do so. There is no such thing as a private faith.

Christianity is not a crutch. It is a cross. Resolve today to follow Him.

Prayer:

Ask for the help of His Holy Spirit to turn your back on everything that you know is wrong, to take up the cross daily, and unashamedly to follow Christ. You will be joining with millions of others like Paul Schneider and Otto Neururer who have taken up their crosses and followed Christ and as a result have made an impact on the community around them.

Warnings and Encouragements

12 Meanwhile, when a crowd of many thousands had gathered, so that they were trampling on one another, Jesus began to speak first to his disciples, saying: "Be on your guard against the yeast of the Pharisees, which is hypocrisy. ²There is nothing concealed that will not be disclosed, or hidden that will not be made known. ³What you have said in the dark will be heard in the daylight, and what you have whispered in the ear in the inner rooms will be proclaimed from the roofs.

⁴"I tell you, my friends, do not be afraid of those who kill the body and after that can do no more. ⁵But I will show you whom you should fear: Fear him who, after the killing of the body, has power to throw you into hell. Yes, I tell you, fear him. ⁶Are not five sparrows sold for two pennies ? Yet not one of them is forgotten by God. ⁷Indeed, the very hairs of your head are all numbered. Don't be afraid; you are worth more than many sparrows.

⁸"I tell you, whoever acknowledges me before men, the Son of Man will also acknowledge him before the angels of God. ⁹But he who disowns me before men will be disowned before the angels of God. ¹⁰And everyone who speaks a word against the Son of Man will be forgiven, but anyone who blasphemes against the Holy Spirit will not be forgiven.

¹¹"When you are brought before synagogues, rulers and authorities, do not worry about how you will defend yourselves or what you will say, ¹²for the Holy Spirit will teach you at that time what you should say."

The Parable of the Rich Fool

¹³Someone in the crowd said to him, "Teacher, tell my brother to divide the inheritance with me."

¹⁴Jesus replied, "Man, who appointed me a judge or an arbiter between you?" ¹⁵Then he said to them, "Watch out! Be on your guard against all kinds of greed; a man's life does not consist in the abundance of his possessions."

¹⁶And he told them this parable: "The ground of a certain rich man produced a good crop. ¹⁷He thought to himself, 'What shall I do? I have no place to store my crops.'

¹⁸"Then he said, 'This is what I'll do. I will tear down my barns and build bigger ones, and there I will store all my grain and my goods. ¹⁹And I'll say to myself, "You have plenty of good things laid up for many years. Take life easy; eat, drink and be merry." '

²⁰"But God said to him, 'You fool! This very night your life will be demanded from you. Then who will get what you have prepared for yourself?'

²¹"This is how it will be with anyone who stores up things for himself but is not rich toward God."

Do Not Worry

²²Then Jesus said to his disciples: "Therefore I tell you, do not worry about your life, what you will eat; or about your body, what you will wear. ²³Life is more than food, and the body more than clothes. ²⁴Consider the ravens: They do not sow or reap, they have no storeroom or barn; yet God feeds them. And how much more valuable you are than birds! ²⁵Who of you by worrying can add a single hour to his life? ²⁶Since you cannot do this very little thing, why do you worry about the rest?

²⁷"Consider how the lilies grow. They do not labor or spin. Yet I tell you, not even Solomon in all his splendor was dressed like one of these. ²⁸If that is how God clothes the grass of the field, which is here today, and tomorrow is thrown into the fire, how much more will he clothe you, O you of little faith!

Be Prepared

When Ludwig Nobel died in 1888, a journalist, who mistakenly identified the deceased as Alfred Bernard Nobel, wrote and published his obituary instead. There, in the newspaper, Alfred Bernard Nobel was able to see written before him a summary of the achievements of his life. Materially, it had been a great success—Alfred was very rich. He was a scientific genius; he invented dynamite together with the even more potent solution, blasting gelatin, and in 1880 he patented an almost smokeless gun powder that European armies rushed to buy. In this newspaper obituary he was described as "the merchant of death." But Alfred Nobel was shocked. Was this all his life had been about? Enabling humankind to destroy itself more efficiently?

This startling incident caused Alfred Bernard Nobel to work for world peace. He also re-wrote his will. He instructed his executors that, when he did die, to convert all his remaining property to cash (it came to $9 million) and to invest it in safe securities, the interest from which would be awarded annually in five prizes to those persons who had contributed most to the benefit of humankind during the preceding year. The five categories were physics, chemistry, medicine, literature, and peace. Alfred Nobel died on November 10, 1896. Since then over 600 Nobel Laureates have been recognized.

If you died today what would your obituary say?

Here Jesus tells a story about another "successful" man—a businessman who had made a lot of money, was considering plans for expanding his company, and was looking forward to the prospect of early retirement. Jesus' hearers would have been basking in this tale of wealth and success but Jesus tells us that his obituary was written by God. It was very short—just "You fool!" The Greek word for "fool" literally means someone "without thought." Although the wealthy man planned, he did not think about the really important questions of life. Here are three aspects of life he failed to consider.

1. He did not think about his long-term future

This man made two mistakes about the length of his life. First, he assumed he had "many years" to live (vs. 19).

In fact he was to die "this very night" (vs. 20)—and would be required to give an account of his life.

Yet he had never thought beyond this life. In counting on time here, he forgot about eternity. So many people take such a short-term view. A wise person takes a long-term view.

2. He did not think about the meaning of life

He thought that life was all about having the hallmarks of success: treasure, leisure, and pleasure (vs. 19).

Treasure

Jesus points out: "Life does not consist in the abundance of . . . possessions" (vs. 15). Material prosperity does not satisfy and does not last (vs. 20).

Leisure

He had planned to "take life easy." Leisure is a blessing but it does not give meaning to life.

Pleasure

He was going to "eat, drink, and be merry." Again, this well-tried combination never truly satisfies. Life is all about a relationship with God through Jesus Christ and our relationships with others.

There is nothing wrong with material possessions, playing a lot of golf, or enjoying our food and drink, but these are not what life is really about—and all of them make absurd ultimate goals.

3. He did not think about his greatest need

The words "I," "my," and "myself" appear 11 times in verses 17-19. The fool thought he was self-sufficient. He thought he could do it by himself: he didn't need God or anyone else. Actually, he was very self-centered. Self-centeredness is the root of the human problem. This is why Jesus came to set us free from the cell of our own self-centeredness.

It is worth asking ourselves these questions:

Do we assume that we have "many years" or are we ready to meet God today?

What is our perspective? Is it this life or eternity?

What are our priorities? Are they treasure, leisure, and pleasure or our relationship with God and loving others?

What is our greatest problem? Do we see our own selfishness and need for forgiveness?

Prayer:

Lord, save me from becoming self-centered. Help me to keep my focus on serving You.

Bible Passage
Luke 14:15-24

[10]But when you are invited, take the lowest place, so that when your host comes, he will say to you, 'Friend, move up to a better place.' Then you will be honored in the presence of all your fellow guests. [11]For everyone who exalts himself will be humbled, and he who humbles himself will be exalted."

[12]Then Jesus said to his host, "When you give a luncheon or dinner, do not invite your friends, your brothers or relatives, or your rich neighbors; if you do, they may invite you back and so you will be repaid. [13]But when you give a banquet, invite the poor, the crippled, the lame, the blind, [14]and you will be blessed. Although they cannot repay you, you will be repaid at the resurrection of the righteous."

The Parable of the Great Banquet
[15]**When one of those at the table with him heard this, he said to Jesus, "Blessed is the man who will eat at the feast in the kingdom of God."**

[16]**Jesus replied: "A certain man was preparing a great banquet and invited many guests. [17]At the time of the banquet he sent his servant to tell those who had been invited, 'Come, for everything is now ready.'**

[18]**But they all alike began to make excuses. The first said, 'I have just bought a field, and I must go and see it. Please excuse me.'**

[19]**"Another said, 'I have just bought five yoke of oxen, and I'm on my way to try them out. Please excuse me.'**

[20]**"Still another said, 'I just got married, so I can't come.'**

[21]**"The servant came back and reported this to his master. Then the owner of the house became angry and ordered his servant, 'Go out quickly into the streets and alleys of the town and bring in the poor, the crippled,** the blind and the lame.'

[22]**" 'Sir,' the servant said, 'what you ordered has been done, but there is still room.'**

[23]**"Then the master told his servant, 'Go out to the roads and country lanes and make them come in, so that my house will be full. [24]I tell you, not one of those men who were invited will get a taste of my banquet.' "**

The Cost of Being a Disciple
[25]Large crowds were traveling with Jesus, and turning to them he said: [26]"If anyone comes to me and does not hate his father and mother, his wife and children, his brothers and sisters—yes, even his own life—he cannot be my disciple. [27]And anyone who does not carry his cross and follow me cannot be my disciple.

[28]"Suppose one of you wants to build a tower. Will he not first sit down and estimate the cost to see if he has enough money to complete it? [29]For if he lays the foundation and is not able to finish it, everyone who sees it will ridicule him, [30]saying, 'This fellow began to build and was not able to finish.'

[31]"Or suppose a king is about to go to war against another king. Will he not first sit down and consider whether he is able with ten thousand men to oppose the one coming against him with twenty thousand? [32]If he is not able, he will send a delegation while the other is still a long way off and will ask for terms of peace. [33]In the same way, any of you who does not give up everything he has cannot be my disciple.

[34]"Salt is good, but if it loses its saltiness, how can it be made salty again? [35]It is fit neither for the soil nor for the manure pile; it is thrown out.

He who has ears to hear, let him hear."

Excuses

Imagine receiving an invitation to dinner from the President of the United States or one of your state's senators. Supposing we were to reply, "So sorry, I can't make it—I have moved into a new office and I want to go take a look at it." Or, "So sorry, I have bought a new car and I want to try it out." Or, "So sorry, we have recently celebrated our first wedding anniversary—so we can't come." What a missed opportunity! The excuses in verses 18-20 are just like that, irrational and absurd. That is the point. There are different arguments but similar intentions. There is no urgency to look at the field (vs. 18) or try out the oxen (vs. 19), and this man could have brought any number of his friends and relatives (vs. 20).

1. What is the banquet?

Jesus is saying that the Christian life (life in the kingdom of God) is like a banquet. He himself is the host and we experience the lavish hospitality and love of God through Him. The other guests are fellow members of the kingdom. So here we experience not only God's love but the love of other Christians as well. We find meaning and purpose in knowing God. We find life beyond death. Our hunger for forgiveness is satisfied. The Holy Spirit provides the only truly satisfying spiritual drink (John 7:37).

2. Why should anyone not want to be at this party?

In the story Jesus told, all the guests say they are "too busy." For some it is their work, for others their possessions, and for still others it is relationships. Today, people make equally absurd excuses.

"I have no need of God"

When people say this, they usually mean that they are quite happy without God. What they fail to realize is that our greatest need is not happiness but forgiveness. It takes a very proud person to say that they have no need of forgiveness.

Either we accept what Jesus has done for us on the cross, or else one day we will pay the just penalty ourselves for the things we have done wrong.

"There is too much to give up"

Sometimes, God puts His finger on an area of our lives which we know is wrong and we realize that we would have to give things up in order to enjoy this relationship with God through Jesus.

But we need to remember:

a) God loves us. He asks us only to give up things which do us harm. If I saw some small children playing with a carving knife I would tell them to stop, not simply to ruin their fun but to stop them from getting hurt.

b) What we give up is nothing compared to what we receive. The cost of not becoming a Christian is far greater than the cost of becoming a Christian.

c) What we give up is nothing compared to what Jesus gave up for us when He died on the cross for us.

"There must be a catch"

Sometimes people find it hard to accept that there is anything free in this life. They think it all sounds too easy; there must be some hidden catch. However, what they fail to realize is that although it is free for us, it was not free for Jesus. He paid for it with His own blood. It may be easy for us. But it was not easy for Him.

"I'm not good enough"

Not one of us is good enough. Nor can we ever make ourselves good enough for God. But that is why Jesus came. He made it possible for God to accept us just as we are, whatever we have done and however much of a mess we have made of our lives.

"I could never keep it up"

We are right to think we could never keep it up—we cannot by ourselves. But the Spirit of God, who comes to live within us, gives us the power and the strength to keep going as Christians.

"I'll do it later"

This is perhaps the most common excuse. Sometimes people say, "I know it's true—but I am not ready." They put it off. The longer we put it off the harder it becomes and the more we miss out. We never know whether we will get another opportunity. Speaking for myself, my only regret is that I did not accept the gift earlier.

3. How do we get to the banquet?

There is both an invitation—"Come, for everything is now ready"—(vs. 17) and a command—"Make them come in" (vs. 23). It is the love of Christ that draws us to Himself (2 Corinthians 5:14). What do we have to do to accept the invitation?

Change our minds

This is the meaning of the word repentance. If we have not accepted the invitation before, we need to say, "I am sorry. I have made a mistake. I have changed my mind and I want to come."

Accept

Thank Jesus that He has made abundant and eternal life possible through the cross, and put your trust in Him.

Come and receive

Come to the banquet. Come and meet the host, Jesus Christ.
Come and eat and drink. Be filled with the Holy Spirit.
If you have not yet come to the banquet and want to, here is a prayer you could pray.

Prayer:

Lord Jesus Christ,
I am sorry for the things I have done wrong in my life (take a few moments to ask His forgiveness for anything particular that is on your conscience). Please forgive me. I now turn from everything which I know is wrong.
Thank You that You died on the cross for me so that I could be forgiven and set free.
Thank You that You offer me forgiveness and the gift of Your Spirit. I now receive that gift.
Please come into my life by Your Holy Spirit to be with me forever.
Thank You, Lord Jesus. Amen.

The Parable of the Lost Coin

⁸"Or suppose a woman has ten silver coins and loses one. Does she not light a lamp, sweep the house and search carefully until she finds it? ⁹And when she finds it, she calls her friends and neighbors together and says, 'Rejoice with me; I have found my lost coin.' ¹⁰In the same way, I tell you, there is rejoicing in the presence of the angels of God over one sinner who repents."

The Parable of the Lost Son

¹¹Jesus continued: "There was a man who had two sons. ¹²The younger one said to his father, 'Father, give me my share of the estate.' So he divided his property between them.

¹³"Not long after that, the younger son got together all he had, set off for a distant country and there squandered his wealth in wild living. ¹⁴After he had spent everything, there was a severe famine in that whole country, and he began to be in need. ¹⁵So he went and hired himself out to a citizen of that country, who sent him to his fields to feed pigs. ¹⁶He longed to fill his stomach with the pods that the pigs were eating, but no one gave him anything.

¹⁷"When he came to his senses, he said, 'How many of my father's hired men have food to spare, and here I am starving to death! ¹⁸I will set out and go back to my father and say to him: Father, I have sinned against heaven and against you. ¹⁹I am no longer worthy to be called your son; make me like one of your hired men.' ²⁰So he got up and went to his father.

But while he was still a long way off, his father saw him and was filled with compassion for him; he ran to his son, threw his arms around him and kissed him.

²¹"The son said to him, 'Father, I have sinned against heaven and against you. I am no longer worthy to be called your son.'

²²"But the father said to his servants, 'Quick! Bring the best robe and put it on him. Put a ring on his finger and sandals on his feet. ²³Bring the fattened calf and kill it. Let's have a feast and celebrate. ²⁴For this son of mine was dead and is alive again; he was lost and is found.' So they began to celebrate.

²⁵"Meanwhile, the older son was in the field. When he came near the house, he heard music and dancing. ²⁶So he called one of the servants and asked him what was going on. ²⁷'Your brother has come,' he replied, 'and your father has killed the fattened calf because he has him back safe and sound.'

²⁸"The older brother became angry and refused to go in. So his father went out and pleaded with him. ²⁹But he answered his father, 'Look! All these years I've been slaving for you and never disobeyed your orders. Yet you never gave me even a young goat so I could celebrate with my friends. ³⁰But when this son of yours who has squandered your property with prostitutes comes home, you kill the fattened calf for him!'

³¹" 'My son,' the father said, 'you are always with me, and everything I have is yours. ³²But we had to celebrate and be glad, because this brother of yours was dead and is alive again; he was lost and is found.' "

The Parable of the Shrewd Manager

16Jesus told his disciples: "There was a rich man whose manager was accused of wasting his possessions. ²So he called him in and asked him, 'What is this I hear about you? Give an account of your management, because you cannot be manager any longer.'

³"The manager said to himself, 'What shall I do now? My master is taking away my job. I'm not strong enough to dig, and I'm ashamed to beg— ⁴I know what I'll do so that, when I lose my job here, people will welcome me into their houses.'

The Drama of Life

This has been called "the greatest short story ever told." Jesus chose to tell it to a group of people who had yet to make up their minds about God. In the story the father represents God and the two sons represent you and me. It applies to those who have drifted away from God as well as to those who have never known such a relationship. We can think of it as the drama of life in three acts.

Act I—The Search for Fulfillment (vss. 11-12)

Scene I—The "give me" mentality (vs. 12)

The younger son asks to see his father. He already has a share of the estate (vs. 12). He has the use of the income. He will receive the rest of it on his father's death, but he says, "I want my inheritance now." He is saying in effect: "I don't want anyone else telling me what to do" and so he breaks the relationship with his father. Christianity is about a relationship with God. When we say, "I can lead my life without God. I don't need You. I don't want You," we break that relationship. The father lets him go just as God lets us go.

Scene II—Fleeting pleasures (vs. 13)

He collects "all he had" (vs. 13). For this son life never seems better. He sees the potential and the opportunities and with a tremor of excitement, he sets off for the Las Vegas of the ancient world with its night clubs, brothels, and gambling dens. He leads a "wild" life (vs. 13), but his pleasure is very temporary. He is wasting his life as he "squandered his wealth" (vs. 13).

Scene III—Life without God (vss. 14-16)

Sense of emptiness

He has "spent everything" (vs. 14). He begins to "be in need" (vs. 14).

Loss of freedom

He looked for freedom but has found slavery (vs. 15). He has ended up feeding pigs—an occupation forbidden to the Jews since pigs were regarded as "unclean."

Hunger

He longs to fill his stomach with the pods that the pigs eat (vs. 16). This is a picture of the hunger deep in our hearts, which can only be satisfied by a relationship with God.

Loneliness

When he had money, he had friends and was surrounded by people. But they deserted him when he was broke. They didn't really care about him as a true friend.

When he had money to spend he was all right, but now "no one gives him anything" (vs. 16b).

Act II—In the Valley of Decision (vss. 17-20a)

He starts to do some thinking

"He came to his senses" (vs. 17). This means literally that "he came back to himself." He uses his mind and realizes where he should have been all along: with his father.

Following Jesus and becoming a Christian is not an irrational leap of faith. It is the most rational thing that we can do. Running away from the facts is irrational and will lead nowhere.

He doesn't worry about his motives

He wants food (vs. 17). We will never get our motives right. What matters is doing the right thing.

He plans to change his ways

It is very hard to admit that we are wrong—we all fear losing face. When he left he said, "Give me." Now he says, "Forgive me" (vss. 18-19).

He does something

"He got up and went to his father" (vs. 20). Faith involves a decision. It is an act of the will based on what we know.

Act III—Coming Home (vss. 20b-24)

The son has left home and forgotten about his father but the father has not forgotten about his son (vs. 20b). Every day he watches, waits, and hopes. When he sees him he is "filled with compassion" (vs. 20b). It breaks his heart to see the mess his son has made of his life. "He runs" (vs. 20b). For an elderly middle-eastern man it was not considered dignified to run, but he is not worried about his dignity. He throws his arms around him and kisses him many times.

The son starts his confession (vs. 21) but the father interrupts. There is no rebuke or reproach, no "I told you so," no conditions. He says, "Quick!" (vs. 22). He gives him the best robe reserved for honored guests and a ring, a sign of confidence and distinction. He gives him shoes. Slaves and even guests did not wear shoes, only the master and his sons. They are a sign of forgiveness and reinstatement. He kills the "fattened calf." He throws a party, a feast, a celebration with music and dancing (vs. 25). This is a picture of the Christian life.

But the elder brother is angry (vs. 28). He has always been around the home but never really seems to have enjoyed his relationship. He can't understand what all the fuss is about and thinks it is all excessive but he is invited to the party as well. He too could enjoy the benefits of total forgiveness, restored relationships, solid joy, and fullness of life.

Don't miss out on the party. Whether you feel more like the younger or the older brother, the key is to get back into a right relationship with the Father and join in the celebrations. If you are not in this relationship you can come home today. Don't worry about your motives.

Prayer:

Pray the prayer the younger son planned to pray (vs. 19). Turn to God as your Father and start to enjoy His great love and generosity toward you.

Bible Passage
Luke 19:1-10

Jesus Again Predicts His Death

³¹Jesus took the Twelve aside and told them, "We are going up to Jerusalem, and everything that is written by the prophets about the Son of Man will be fulfilled. ³²He will be handed over to the Gentiles. They will mock him, insult him, spit on him, flog him and kill him. ³³On the third day he will rise again."

³⁴The disciples did not understand any of this. Its meaning was hidden from them, and they did not know what he was talking about.

A Blind Beggar Receives His Sight

³⁵As Jesus approached Jericho, a blind man was sitting by the roadside begging. ³⁶When he heard the crowd going by, he asked what was happening. ³⁷They told him, "Jesus of Nazareth is passing by."

³⁸He called out, "Jesus, Son of David, have mercy on me!"

³⁹Those who led the way rebuked him and told him to be quiet, but he shouted all the more, "Son of David, have mercy on me!"

⁴⁰Jesus stopped and ordered the man to be brought to him. When he came near, Jesus asked him, ⁴¹"What do you want me to do for you?"

"Lord, I want to see," he replied.

⁴²Jesus said to him, "Receive your sight; your faith has healed you." ⁴³Immediately he received his sight and followed Jesus, praising God. When all the people saw it, they also praised God.

Zacchaeus the Tax Collector

19Jesus entered Jericho and was passing through. ²A man was there by the name of Zacchaeus; he was a chief tax collector and was wealthy. ³He wanted to see who Jesus was, but being a short man he could not, because of the crowd. ⁴So he ran ahead and climbed a sycamore-fig tree to see him, since Jesus was coming that way.

⁵When Jesus reached the spot, he looked up and said to him, "Zacchaeus, come down immediately. I must stay at your house today." ⁶So he came down at once and welcomed him gladly.

⁷All the people saw this and began to mutter, "He has gone to be the guest of a 'sinner.'"

⁸But Zacchaeus stood up and said to the Lord, "Look, Lord! Here and now I give half of my possessions to the poor, and if I have cheated anybody out of anything, I will pay back four times the amount."

⁹Jesus said to him, "Today salvation has come to this house, because this man, too, is a son of Abraham. ¹⁰For the Son of Man came to seek and to save what was lost."

The Parable of the Ten Minas

¹¹While they were listening to this, he went on to tell them a parable, because he was near Jerusalem and the people thought that the kingdom of God was going to appear at once. ¹²He said: "A man of noble birth went to a distant country to have himself appointed king and then to return. ¹³So he called ten of his servants and gave them ten minas. 'Put this money to work,' he said, 'until I come back.'

¹⁴"But his subjects hated him and sent a delegation after him to say, 'We don't want this man to be our king.'

¹⁵"He was made king, however, and returned home. Then he sent for the servants to whom he had given the money, in order to find out what they had gained with it.

¹⁶"The first one came and said, 'Sir, your mina has earned ten more.'

¹⁷"'Well done, my good servant!' his master replied. 'Because you have been trustworthy in a very small matter, take charge of ten cities.'

Mid-Life Crisis

Zacchaeus was probably in mid-life. He was old enough to be at the top of his profession (vs. 2), but young enough to climb a tree (vs. 4). He was a wealthy man. He had the status of being a chief tax collector with people working under him and had no doubt been promoted many times. He had success but at a cost.

"Zacchaeus"

Tax collectors had an appalling reputation for corruption and collaborating with the occupying Roman power. He had worked hard for the sake of his family but they must have faced ostracism owing to his line of work and unpopularity.

His parents had called him Zacchaeus meaning "the righteous one"—but now perhaps he had no time for God. Religious people regarded him as a "sinner" (vs. 7). In the light of all this, perhaps he was facing a mid-life crisis!

1. Why did he want to see Jesus? (vss. 3-4)

Two things he realized:

First, he realized he had a need. Despite all his money and success there was still something missing.

Secondly, he realized that Jesus might provide the key. "He wanted to see who Jesus was" (vs. 3). The most important question we can ever ask is, "Who is Jesus?"

Four things he did not realize:

First, he did not realize that you cannot hide from Jesus. He wanted to see Jesus without Jesus seeing him (vs. 4)—he probably felt guilty. But none of us can hide. Jesus knew him.

He knew his name. For a Hebrew, if someone knew your name, they knew a great deal about you. God knows all about us.

Secondly, he did not realize that Jesus loved him in spite of his sin (Romans 5:8). Jesus picked him out in a crowd. Jesus sees us wherever we are. He was on his way to Jerusalem to die on a cross for us all. He was going to die for Zacchaeus (Galatians 2:20).

Thirdly, he did not realize that Jesus wanted to know him (vs. 5). This is the heart of the Christian faith: knowing Jesus Christ.

Fourthly, he did not realize that Jesus required a response (vs. 5). This is a moment of high drama. Jesus says, "Come down immediately." How was Zacchaeus to respond?

2. How did Zacchaeus respond? (vss. 6-7)

First, he "came down." He obeyed Jesus and humbled himself. Secondly, he did not put it off. He came down "at once." Thirdly, he "welcomed him." Fourthly, he did so "gladly." At last he had found happiness—but in an unexpected way. Fifthly, he was not put off by the crowd's attitude (vs. 7). They were shocked and said in effect, "He is not the religious type." But Zacchaeus didn't care what the people thought.

3. What happened as a result? (vss. 8, 10)

A total transformation took place in Zacchaeus's attitude, his life, his friends and family, and in the society around him.

His attitude

He completely changed his attitude toward his possessions. His experience of Jesus put everything else into perspective. It was no longer, "How much can I get?" but rather, "How much can I give?" (vs. 8). He started to get his life sorted out by paying back what he owed. It was his relationship with Jesus Christ that enabled him to do this.

His life

Zacchaeus had found forgiveness and a totally new start (vs. 9). The mess of the past had been cleared up. He had found freedom from the rat-race. He had discovered that his future was secure through a relationship with Christ which was to go on forever.

His family

Jesus said, "Today salvation has come to this house" (vs. 9).
Everyone in the household was included.

Society

The poor benefited. He gave half his possessions to the poor (vs. 8).
Justice was done: those who had been cheated were repaid.

We don't have to go through a mid-life crisis to receive Jesus. He says
to each of us that He wants to stay at our house today. If you have not yet
done so why not invite Him in today? Ask Him to show you how much
He loves you. Think about the fact that He died for you. Ask Him to show
you if there is anything you need to put right in your life. If there is, why
not follow Zacchaeus's example and do so right away?

Prayer:

You might like to pray the famous prayer that an African girl prayed.

"O great Chief, light a candle within my heart that I may see what is
there and sweep the rubbish from your dwelling place."

[27]If anyone speaks in a tongue, two—or at the most three—should speak, one at a time, and someone must interpret. [28]If there is no interpreter, the speaker should keep quiet in the church and speak to himself and God.

[29]Two or three prophets should speak, and the others should weigh carefully what is said. [30]And if a revelation comes to someone who is sitting down, the first speaker should stop. [31]For you can all prophesy in turn so that everyone may be instructed and encouraged. [32]The spirits of prophets are subject to the control of prophets. [33]For God is not a God of disorder but of peace.

As in all the congregations of the saints, [34]women should remain silent in the churches. They are not allowed to speak, but must be in submission, as the Law says. [35]If they want to inquire about something, they should ask their own husbands at home; for it is disgraceful for a woman to speak in the church.

[36]Did the word of God originate with you? Or are you the only people it has reached? [37]If anybody thinks he is a prophet or spiritually gifted, let him acknowledge that what I am writing to you is the Lord's command. [38]If he ignores this, he himself will be ignored.

[39]Therefore, my brothers, be eager to prophesy, and do not forbid speaking in tongues. [40]But everything should be done in a fitting and orderly way.

The Ressurection of Christ

15 Now, brothers, I want to remind you of the gospel I preached to you, which you received and on which you have taken your stand. [2]By this gospel you are saved, if you hold firmly to the word I preached to you. Otherwise, you have believed in vain.

[3]For what I received I passed on to you as of first importance: that Christ died for our sins according to the Scriptures, [4]that he was buried, that he was raised on the third day according to the Scriptures, [5]and that he appeared to Peter, and then to the Twelve. [6]After that, he appeared to more than five hundred of the brothers at the same time, most of whom are still living, though some have fallen asleep. [7]Then he appeared to James, then to all the apostles, [8]and last of all he appeared to me also, as to one abnormally born.

[9]For I am the least of the apostles and do not even deserve to be called an apostle, because I persecuted the church of God. [10]But by the grace of God I am what I am, and his grace to me was not without effect. No, I worked harder than all of them—yet not I, but the grace of God that was with me. [11]Whether, then, it was I or they, this is what we preach, and this is what you believed.

The Resurrection of the Dead

[12]But if it is preached that Christ has been raised from the dead, how can some of you say that there is no resurrection of the dead? [13]If there is no resurrection of the dead, then not even Christ has been raised. [14]And if Christ has not been raised, our preaching is useless and so is your faith. [15]More than that, we are then found to be false witnesses about God, for we have testified about God that he raised Christ from the dead. But he did not raise him if in fact the dead are not raised. [16]For if the dead are not raised, then Christ has not been raised either. [17]And if Christ has not been raised, your faith is futile; you are still in your sins. [18]Then those also who have fallen asleep in Christ are lost. [19]If only for this life we have hope in Christ, we are to be pitied more than all men.

[20]But Christ has indeed been raised from the dead, the firstfruits of those who have fallen asleep.

What Is the Gospel?

What was the church saying about Jesus three years after He died? The book of Corinthians is an early Christian document. It was written in about 54 A.D. (around 20 years after the events described). However, Paul here appears to be referring to an even earlier record. He speaks of having "received" and "passed on" (vs. 3) the Gospel. These are technical words for receiving and handing on an authorized tradition. We know from elsewhere in the New Testament that he received this tradition within three years of the crucifixion. This may well be the earliest creed of the church. What is its message?

Paul says he wants to remind his readers about the Gospel. The Gospel means good news. It is a message that brings great joy. It is good news about a person. The Corinthians received this news. They took their stand on it (vs. 1) and by it they were "saved" (vs. 2). The modern way of putting that would be to say that they found freedom. What is the message of the Gospel?

1. The Death of Christ (vss. 3-4)

The person

The person who died was the "Christ" (vs. 3)—the Messiah, literally the "anointed one." He was a fully human being but He was more than just another person. He was the Son of God.

The plan

It was no mistake. He died "according to the Scriptures" (vss. 3-4). Jesus is unique in the history of humankind as His life and death were both described up to hundreds of years beforehand.

The purpose

His death was "for our sins" (vs. 3). The good news is that Jesus' death on the cross has made possible the forgiveness of our sins. The weight of our guilt has been removed because He has broken the power of sin, freeing us from every addiction. Every enemy has been defeated. He has disarmed the principalities and powers of evil defeating every possible enemy. We have nothing to fear.

2. The Resurrection of Christ (vss. 4-8)

"He was buried" (vs. 4)

Dying and being buried does not distinguish Him from others. Buddha, Mohammed, Marx, and Lenin died and were buried. But . . .

"He was raised" (vs. 4)

This is the earliest historical reference to the empty tomb. The Greek word for "raised" refers to something that happened in the past but whose effect remains in force. Having been raised by God, Jesus is alive today.

No one else in the history of the world has been "raised" and is still alive.

"He appeared" (vss. 5-8)

Paul does not give an exhaustive list of the appearances but enough to show they were well-attested. He appeared to Peter (Luke 24:34), to the 12 apostles and to over 500 others, then to all the apostles (more than the 12), then to James, the brother of Jesus. Finally, He appeared to Paul, who is writing here his own first-hand account (vs. 8). One day Paul was at the stoning of Stephen, hungry for the blood of Christians, approving his death, destroying the church, dragging Christians off to prison, and breathing out murderous threats against them. Within a few days he was preaching that Jesus was the Son of God (Acts 7:54—9:22).

The resurrection is rooted in history, grounded in Scripture, and confirmed by experience.

The great news for us is that the past has been dealt with. Jesus died for our sins, thereby removing our guilt. The resurrection attests to the achievement of the cross.

Secondly, our future is secure. Death is certain but for the Christian it is only "falling asleep." It is not to be feared. We expect to wake up in the morning. In the rest of 1 Corinthians 15, Paul assures his readers that one day they too will have a resurrection body.

Thirdly, the present takes on a new dimension. Jesus is alive. We can know Him. This is the heart of Christianity: a relationship with a living person who gives meaning and purpose to life. What are we to do? Paul's answer here is that we should receive this news, believe it, hold firmly to it, and pass it on.

Paul received this good news. He passed it on to the Corinthians, they believed it and passed it on. It has since been passed on to us through the centuries. Now it is our turn. We have been entrusted with the message. Our task is to pass it on to our generation in a language that they can understand.

Prayer:

This would be a good moment to thank God for the Gospel. Thank Jesus for dying for you. Thank Him that He is alive and with you. Pray for "the grace of God" (vs. 10) to be with you as you pass on the good news to others that they too might find this freedom.

Bible Passage
Ephesians 1:15-23

1 Paul, an apostle of Christ Jesus by the will of God,

To the saints in Ephesus, the faithful in Christ Jesus:

²Grace and peace to you from God our Father and the Lord Jesus Christ.

Spiritual Blessings in Christ

³Praise be to the God and Father of our Lord Jesus Christ, who has blessed us in the heavenly realms with every spiritual blessing in Christ. ⁴For he chose us in him before the creation of the world to be holy and blameless in his sight. In love ⁵he predestined us to be adopted as his sons through Jesus Christ, in accordance with his pleasure and will— ⁶to the praise of his glorious grace, which he has freely given us in the One he loves. ⁷In him we have redemption through his blood, the forgiveness of sins, in accordance with the riches of God's grace ⁸that he lavished on us with all wisdom and understanding. ⁹And he made known to us the mystery of his will according to his good pleasure, which he purposed in Christ, ¹⁰to be put into effect when the times will have reached their fulfillment—to bring all things in heaven and on earth together under one head, even Christ.

¹¹In him we were also chosen, having been predestined according to the plan of him who works out everything in conformity with the purpose of his will, ¹²in order that we, who were the first to hope in Christ, might be for the praise of his glory. ¹³And you also were included in Christ when you heard the word of truth, the gospel of your salvation. Having believed, you were marked in him with a seal, the promised Holy Spirit, ¹⁴who is a deposit guaranteeing our inheritance until the redemption of those who are God's possession—to the praise of his glory.

Thanksgiving and Prayer

¹⁵For this reason, ever since I heard about your faith in the Lord Jesus and your love for all the saints, ¹⁶I have not stopped giving thanks for you, remembering you in my prayers. ¹⁷I keep asking that the God of our Lord Jesus Christ, the glorious Father, may give you the Spirit of wisdom and revelation, so that you may know him better. ¹⁸I pray also that the eyes of your heart may be enlightened in order that you may know the hope to which he has called you, the riches of his glorious inheritance in the saints, ¹⁹and his incomparably great power for us who believe. That power is like the working of his mighty strength, ²⁰which he exerted in Christ when he raised him from the dead and seated him at his right hand in the heavenly realms, ²¹far above all rule and authority, power and dominion, and every title that can be given, not only in the present age but also in the one to come. ²²And God placed all things under his feet and appointed him to be head over everything for the church, ²³which is his body, the fullness of him who fills everything in every way.

Made Alive in Christ

2 As for you, you were dead in your transgressions and sins, ²in which you used to live when you followed the ways of this world and of the ruler of the kingdom of the air, the spirit who is now at work in those who are disobedient. ³All of us also lived among them at one time, gratifying the cravings of our sinful nature and following its desires and thoughts. Like the rest, we were by nature objects of wrath. ⁴But because of his great love for us, God, who is rich in mercy, ⁵made us alive with Christ even when we were dead in transgressions—it is by grace you have been saved.

Know What You've Got

William Randolph Hearst (1863-1951), on whose life the film Citizen Kane *was based, built up the largest newspaper chain in the United States during the 1920s. He built himself a grandiose castle on a 240,000 acre ranch in California. It contained a vast collection of antiques and* objets d'art *in which he invested a huge fortune. He collected them from all over the world and stored them in warehouses in different places.*

One day he came across the description of a valuable piece of art in a magazine. He was determined to get hold of it, but no one knew where it was. He sent his agent all over the world to find it. Months and months went by. Finally the man came back and reported, "Mr. Hearst, I have found it." With great joy he asked, "Where? Where was it?" He replied, "It was in your warehouse. You bought it years ago."

William Randolph Hearst had been frantically searching for what he already possessed. Many Christians are frantically searching for what they already possess. Paul prays that we might know what we already possess in Christ.

He prays for the Ephesians that they may know four things that they already possess in Christ.

1. The most exciting relationship possible (vs. 17)

The whole Trinity is involved in this relationship: "the glorious Father," "our Lord Jesus Christ," and the "Spirit of wisdom and revelation" who enables us to know God better. This is the purpose for which we were made. This is what gives meaning to life.

Jesus Christ has risen from the dead. The same Jesus who died on the cross is alive and present with us now, as He will be forever. Therefore, any person anywhere at any time has the opportunity to enjoy the same kind of relationship with Him as the disciples had with Him in person about 2000 years ago.

2. A totally secure future (vs. 18b)

So many people are worried about the future. In Christ our future is entirely secure. Paul prays that we might know "the hope to which he has called you."

One young man had recently come to Christ when his mother died. He wrote to me about his experience of the funeral: "I suddenly understood what it meant to be a Christian. In those 30 minutes my eyes were fully opened for the first time. I realized why I had not been racked with grief and bitterness at the loss of my mother—sure I had cried and I was saddened, but I knew—I know—that her faith in Jesus Christ had saved her, and that she would enjoy eternal life.

"I had seen it in her eyes just before she died last Thursday, and yesterday I felt the realization flood through me—warm, rich, and comforting. It was then that I finally understood the enormity of the sacrifice Jesus made for us on the cross, that we really can have eternal life in heaven, through Him."

3. Extraordinary riches (vs. 18b)

Paul prays that we would know "the riches of his glorious inheritance in the saints" (vs. 18). One day we will see God and we will worship Him face to face. We will be together with all who have died in faith and we will have perfect fellowship with one another. There will be a great multitude there with us. We will become like Christ both in our bodies and in our characters. The enjoyment of this inheritance begins now as we get a foretaste of the future.

4. The power of God in us (vs. 19)

Paul refers to "his incomparably great power for us who believe." Power belongs to God but He has come to live in us. As Paul searches for words which will adequately describe this power, he recalls the resurrection and ascension of Jesus.

A public demonstration of the power of God took place in history (vs. 20a). It started in a cemetery with a corpse. The dead body of Jesus was raised. Neither death nor hell nor Satan nor sin nor demons could hold Him.

He ascended (vss. 20b-21). God "seated him at his right hand in the heavenly realms, far above all rule and authority, power and dominion." He was then given "every title that can be given, not only in the present age but also in the one to come."

In this context, "right hand" means the place of highest honor and authority. Here in England, the queen was reminded of this at her coronation. When the orb was placed in her hand, she was told, "When you see this orb set under the cross, remember that the whole world is subject to the power and empire of Christ our Redeemer."

In verse 22a we hear that "God placed all things under his feet." This is a symbol of His sovereignty. It is a metaphor derived from the sphere of warfare: sometimes victorious kings would place their feet on the necks of the defeated enemy (e.g., Joshua 10:24; Isaiah 51:23).

God "appointed him to be head over everything for the church, which is his body, the fullness of him who fills everything in every way." Christ is the head of the Church and the Church is His body. Why is the Church described as the "fullness of him who fills everything in every way"? Because the Church completes Christ in the same way as a body completes a head. But the Church can only function properly if it is constantly being filled with God's power. God's power is available for us, His church. His plans for a united Christian universe is in the hands of the Church.

How big is our vision? Is it simply for our own life? If it is, is that not a little self-centered? Perhaps it stretches to include our family, our friends, our city, maybe our nation, or even the entire world. Paul's vision is for a united Christian universe under the Lordship of Christ. The Church is God's instrument for achieving this. We can never rest in this life until that

"my life is hard enough without a vision for other peoples."

is complete. We cannot rest while there is widespread poverty, appalling third world debt, rising crime rates, and so on.

It is no good saying, "We can't do anything." Paul prays that we would see the potential we have in Christ. He prays that we would get to know Him better and thus start to see our individual and collective calling, our inheritance and the power He has given us to move forward from where we are now to where God would like us to be. Do we see the task that God has entrusted to His church? We cannot rest until the whole universe is subject to his reign—"the fullness of him who fills everything in every way."

Prayer:

This is a good moment to thank God for everything He has given us, and which we already possess in Christ. We could thank Him for our relationship with Him, for the hope that He gives us, for His promised inheritance, for the fact that He raised Jesus from the dead and that the same power is available for us now.

Thanksgiving and Prayer

[15]For this reason, ever since I heard about your faith in the Lord Jesus and your love for all the saints, [16]I have not stopped giving thanks for you, remembering you in my prayers. [17]I keep asking that the God of our Lord Jesus Christ, the glorious Father, may give you the Spirit of wisdom and revelation, so that you may know him better. [18]I pray also that the eyes of your heart may be enlightened in order that you may know the hope to which he has called you, the riches of his glorious inheritance in the saints, [19]and his incomparably great power for us who believe. That power is like the working of his mighty strength, [20]which he exerted in Christ when he raised him from the dead and seated him at his right hand in the heavenly realms, [21]far above all rule and authority, power and dominion, and every title that can be given, not only in the present age but also in the one to come. [22]And God placed all things under his feet and appointed him to be head over everything for the church, [23]which is his body, the fullness of him who fills everything in every way.

Made Alive in Christ

2 As for you, you were dead in your transgressions and sins, [2]in which you used to live when you followed the ways of this world and of the ruler of the kingdom of the air, the spirit who is now at work in those who are disobedient. [3]All of us also lived among them at one time, gratifying the cravings of our sinful nature and following its desires and thoughts. Like the rest, we were by nature objects of wrath. [4]But because of his great love for us, God, who is rich in mercy, [5]made us alive with Christ even when we were dead in transgressions—it is by grace you have been saved. [6]And God raised us up with Christ and seated us with him in the heavenly realms in Christ Jesus, [7]in order that in the coming ages he might show the incomparable riches of his grace, expressed in his kindness to us in Christ Jesus. [8]For it is by grace you have been saved, through faith—and this not from yourselves, it is the gift of God— [9]not by works, so that no one can boast. [10]For we are God's workmanship, created in Christ Jesus to do good works, which God prepared in advance for us to do.

One in Christ

[11]Therefore, remember that formerly you who are Gentiles by birth and called "uncircumcised" by those who call themselves "the circumcision" (that done in the body by the hands of men)— [12]remember that at that time you were separate from Christ, excluded from citizenship in Israel and foreigners to the covenants of the promise, without hope and without God in the world. [13]But now in Christ Jesus you who once were far away have been brought near through the blood of Christ.

[14]For he himself is our peace, who has made the two one and has destroyed the barrier, the dividing wall of hostility, [15]by abolishing in his flesh the law with its commandments and regulations. His purpose was to create in himself one new man out of the two, thus making peace, [16]and in this one body to reconcile both of them to God through the cross, by which he put to death their hostility. [17]He came and preached peace to you who were far away and peace to those who were near. [18]For through him we both have access to the Father by one Spirit.

[19]Consequently, you are no longer foreigners and aliens, but fellow citizens with God's people and members of God's household, [20]built on the foundation of the apostles and prophets, with Christ Jesus himself as the chief cornerstone. [21]In him the whole building is joined together and rises to become a holy temple in the Lord.

Rescued

If you go into a jewelry shop and you want a diamond ring, the jeweler lays a black velvet cloth on the counter. Then the diamond ring is placed right in the middle of that black cloth. Against the black background the diamond sparkles in all its beauty. Similarly, we cannot see the wonder and wealth of God's love until we see it against the backdrop of our sin.

1. What have we been rescued from? (vss. 1-3)

Death (vs. 1)

We were as dead and unresponsive as a corpse. We did not recognize the love of God, the identity of Jesus, or the power of the Holy Spirit. We were intended to live in a relationship with God but two things broke that relationship: our trespasses (times when we crossed God's boundaries and did what we knew to be wrong) and our sins (where we fell short and failed to do what we should have done).

Disobedience (vss. 2-3)

When we have no relationship with God we act as everybody else seems to be acting. We follow "the ways of this world" (vs. 2). In this context, "world" means society organized without reference to God. The devil (vs. 2b) controls the lives of those who are disobedient to God, encouraging them to follow the instincts of their sinful nature. It is easy to find oneself enslaved by the world, the flesh, and the devil.

Doom (vs. 3)

We were "by nature objects of wrath." We have all been found guilty, and guilt requires a sentence. "Wrath" means righteous anger. It is God's personal, righteous, constant hostility to evil. It is the inevitable reaction of a holy God to sin.

The diagnosis is as bad as it possibly could be. This is the condition of every man and woman without Christ. A dead person can do nothing to make themselves alive.

2. How have we been rescued? (vss. 4-9)

What has God done?

Two of the greatest words in the Bible are: "But . . . God" (vs. 4). The rescue came by God's initiative because He loves us so much. It was a result of "his great love." From the first page of the Bible to the last the message is that "God loves you."

The rescue—the crucifixion of Christ—arose out of God's mercy. He is "rich in mercy," full of forgiveness and grace.

What can we do?

Paul makes two negative points. First, we cannot save ourselves (vs. 8). We cannot contribute to our rescue. Second, it is not "by works" (vs. 9). We cannot save ourselves by our own efforts and achievements.

Then he makes two positive points. First, it is "by grace" (vs. 8). It is God's free and undeserved mercy to us. The children's definition of grace is "**G**od's **R**iches **A**t **C**hrist's **E**xpense." Second, it is "through faith" (vs. 8). It is a gift. We can only say, "Thank You." We do not earn it by our faith. Faith is the way in which we receive the gift.

3. What are we rescued for? (vss. 5-10)

Resurrection (vs. 5)

We are no longer dead but "made alive" (vs. 5). We are "raised up with Christ and seated . . . in the heavenly realms" (vs. 6). Christ's own bodily resurrection points the way to our own.

Future hope (vs. 7)

We are no longer facing judgment but have the most exciting future hope, to enjoy God's kindness for all eternity—"the incomparable riches of his grace, expressed in his kindness to us in Christ Jesus" (vs. 7).

Prepared Plan (vs. 10)

God has prepared in advance "good works" for us to do. Paul whole-heartedly repudiated good works as grounds for salvation but whole-heartedly insisted on them as the fruit of it.

Prayer:

We should continue to thank God for all He has done for us—for His great love, His mercy, and His grace. Thank Him for His rescue, His kindness, for the "riches of his grace" and the plan He has for your future. Pray for His guidance and help as you seek to do the "good works" He has prepared for you to do.

³⁵The Father loves the Son and has placed everything in his hands. ³⁶Whoever believes in the Son has eternal life, but whoever rejects the Son will not see life, for God's wrath remains on him."

Jesus Talks With a Samaritan Woman

4 The Pharisees heard that Jesus was gaining and baptizing more disciples than John, ²although in fact it was not Jesus who baptized, but his disciples. ³When the Lord learned of this, he left Judea and went back once more to Galilee.

⁴Now he had to go through Samaria. ⁵So he came to a town in Samaria called Sychar, near the plot of ground Jacob had given to his son Joseph. ⁶Jacob's well was there, and Jesus, tired as he was from the journey, sat down by the well. It was about the sixth hour.

⁷When a Samaritan woman came to draw water, Jesus said to her, "Will you give me a drink?" ⁸(His disciples had gone into the town to buy food.)

⁹The Samaritan woman said to him, "You are a Jew and I am a Samaritan woman. How can you ask me for a drink?" (For Jews do not associate with Samaritans.)

¹⁰Jesus answered her, "If you knew the gift of God and who it is that asks you for a drink, you would have asked him and he would have given you living water."

¹¹"Sir," the woman said, "you have nothing to draw with and the well is deep. Where can you get this living water? ¹²Are you greater than our father Jacob, who gave us the well and drank from it himself, as did also his sons and his flocks and herds?"

¹³Jesus answered, "Everyone who drinks this water will be thirsty again, ¹⁴but whoever drinks the water I give him will never thirst. Indeed, the water I give him will become in him a spring of water welling up to eternal life."

¹⁵The woman said to him, "Sir, give me this water so that I won't get thirsty and have to keep coming here to draw water."

¹⁶He told her, "Go, call your husband and come back."

¹⁷"I have no husband," she replied.

Jesus said to her, "You are right when you say you have no husband. ¹⁸The fact is, you have had five husbands, and the man you now have is not your husband. What you have just said is quite true."

¹⁹"Sir," the woman said, "I can see that you are a prophet. ²⁰Our fathers worshiped on this mountain, but you Jews claim that the place where we must worship is in Jerusalem."

²¹Jesus declared, "Believe me, woman, a time is coming when you will worship the Father neither on this mountain nor in Jerusalem. ²²You Samaritans worship what you do not know; we worship what we do know, for salvation is from the Jews. ²³Yet a time is coming and has now come when the true worshipers will worship the Father in spirit and truth, for they are the kind of worshipers the Father seeks. ²⁴God is spirit, and his worshipers must worship in spirit and in truth."

²⁵The woman said, "I know that Messiah" (called Christ) "is coming. When he comes, he will explain everything to us."

²⁶Then Jesus declared, "I who speak to you am he."

The Disciples Rejoin Jesus

²⁷Just then his disciples returned and were surprised to find him talking with a woman. But no one asked, "What do you want?" or "Why are you talking with her?"

²⁸Then, leaving her water jar, the woman went back to the town and said to the people, ²⁹"Come, see a man who told me everything I ever did. Could this be the Christ?" ³⁰They came out of the town and made their way toward him.

This Is Your Life

In the U.K. version of the television program "This Is Your Life" a person's life is revealed by the host, Michael Aspel. In this account (and without the help of a team of researchers!) a woman's life is revealed by Jesus Christ. This is one of the most amazing conversations that has ever taken place and it sends the woman rushing back to her town saying to people, "Come, see a man who told me everything I ever did" (vs. 29).

1. Who is this?

Some say Jesus is just a good religious teacher. But Jesus claims to be far more than that. When the conversation turns to the subject of the Messiah, Jesus categorically declares: "I who speak to you am he" (vs. 26). When He starts to speak metaphorically of living water, He is claiming to be the one who can answer her deepest needs (vss. 10, 13-14). John later explains that this water is the Holy Spirit "whom those who believed in him were later to receive" (John 7:39).

Others see Jesus as some distant God—but this passage emphasizes His humanity. He could be hot, tired, thirsty, and hungry. He is certainly not remote. He understands how hard life can be. While living on earth He knew what it was like to have no money, to be hungry, to live without a roof over His head, to be in physical pain, tortured, and rejected by His friends. This is the person who was able to help the Samaritan woman, and is able to help us today.

2. What is He like?

Jesus is the most loving person who has ever lived. In this passage we see the warmth of His love. He broke all the conventions of His time. First, He broke the rabbinic rules by speaking to a woman in public. Second, He broke the barriers of race (vs. 9). The Samaritans were regarded as half-breeds and hated. People would walk 70 miles out of their way to avoid contact with them. Although she was a Samaritan Jesus spoke to her. Third, He broke the barriers of lifestyle. Jesus was, among other things, a Jewish religious teacher. She was a sexually promiscuous woman. The religious did not mix with sinners. But the love of Jesus Christ broke down every barrier.

3. What does He offer?

Well water percolates but then gathers in a stagnant pool. In contrast, Jesus offers "a spring of water" (vs. 14), meaning bubbling, running water. He contrasts well water and spring water. He also contrasts the physical with the spiritual. This (spiritual) water wells up to eternal life (vs. 14). So He also contrasts the short- and long-term. We drink physical water knowing that we will be thirsty again, but this is living, loving, lasting water. Nothing else can satisfy us into eternity. We can appear to be satisfied by materialism, pleasure or status, but none of them truly satisfy.

There is more to life than money, possessions, work, sport, fame, and even human relationships. The woman had tried to gain fulfillment through human relationships, and they did not satisfy. Only a relationship with God through Jesus Christ with the Spirit of God living within us can provide us with the water that satisfies.

4. How did she react?

Her life is a mess underneath the surface (like most of our lives)—see verses 16-18. She reacts in an extraordinary way. She attempts to divert His attention away from her and starts talking about mountains (vss. 19-20).

Perhaps she did not want to face up to the reality of her life: the broken relationships, emptiness, and guilt. Perhaps she felt she had fallen too far. But Jesus came to die for all of us, whatever we have done, and His death on a cross makes forgiveness for everyone possible.

5. What does Jesus do?

Through Jesus her life is transformed. She receives forgiveness for the past. She receives new life in the present and new life for the future—eternal life. Through an ordinary encounter Jesus changed many people's lives forever. He still loves

"In summer you can climb the west face, and even take a picnic. Um, its made of granite, and is dark grey...

to do this today by giving people the "gift of God" (vs. 10): a new and satisfying life which lasts.

Prayer:

We can receive this gift too. If you would like to, speak to Jesus saying you're sorry for your past lived without Him, thanking Him for the gift of new life and asking Him to give you now the living water.

Ask Him to fill you to overflowing. He promises that if we ask Him, God will give us this "living water" (vs. 10). This water will become in you "a spring of water welling up to eternal life" (vs. 14).

²¹Once more Jesus said to them, "I am going away, and you will look for me, and you will die in your sin. Where I go, you cannot come."

²²This made the Jews ask, "Will he kill himself? Is that why he says, 'Where I go, you cannot come'?"

²³But he continued, "You are from below; I am from above. You are of this world; I am not of this world. ²⁴I told you that you would die in your sins; if you do not believe that I am the one I claim to be, you will indeed die in your sins."

²⁵"Who are you?" they asked.

"Just what I have been claiming all along," Jesus replied. ²⁶"I have much to say in judgment of you. But he who sent me is reliable, and what I have heard from him I tell the world."

²⁷They did not understand that he was telling them about his Father. ²⁸So Jesus said, "When you have lifted up the Son of Man, then you will know that I am the one I claim to be and that I do nothing on my own but speak just what the Father has taught me. ²⁹The one who sent me is with me; he has not left me alone, for I always do what pleases him." ³⁰Even as he spoke, many put their faith in him.

The Children of Abraham

³¹**To the Jews who had believed him, Jesus said, "If you hold to my teaching, you are really my disciples. ³²Then you will know the truth, and the truth will set you free."**

³³**They answered him, "We are Abraham's descendants and have never been slaves of anyone. How can you say that we shall be set free?"**

³⁴**Jesus replied, "I tell you the truth, everyone who sins is a slave to sin. ³⁵Now a slave has no permanent place in the family, but a son belongs to it forever. ³⁶So if the Son sets you free, you will be free indeed.** ³⁷I know you are Abraham's descendants. Yet you are ready to kill me, because you

have no room for my word. ³⁸I am telling you what I have seen in the Father's presence, and you do what you have heard from your father."

³⁹"Abraham is our father," they answered.

If you were Abraham's children," said Jesus, "then you would do the things Abraham did. ⁴⁰As it is, you are determined to kill me, a man who has told you the truth that I heard from God. Abraham did not do such things. ⁴¹You are doing the things your own father does."

"We are not illegitimate children," they protested. "The only Father we have is God himself."

The Children of the Devil

⁴²Jesus said to them, "If God were your Father, you would love me, for I came from God and now am here. I have not come on my own; but he sent me. ⁴³Why is my language not clear to you? Because you are unable to hear what I say. ⁴⁴You belong to your father, the devil, and you want to carry out your father's desire. He was a murderer from the beginning, not holding to the truth, for there is no truth in him. When he lies, he speaks his native language, for he is a liar and the father of lies. ⁴⁵Yet because I tell the truth, you do not believe me! ⁴⁶Can any of you prove me guilty of sin? If I am telling the truth, why don't you believe me? ⁴⁷He who belongs to God hears what God says. The reason you do not hear is that you do not belong to God."

The Claims of Jesus About Himself

⁴⁸The Jews answered him, "Aren't we right in saying that you are a Samaritan and demon-possessed?"

⁴⁹"I am not possessed by a demon," said Jesus, "but I honor my Father and you dishonor me. ⁵⁰I am not seeking glory for myself; but there is one who seeks it, and he is the judge.

True Freedom

There are many different forms of freedom. There is national freedom: a country is free from being governed by another country. There is political freedom, including free speech, worship, elections, movement, and a free press. There is racial freedom, the freedom from racial discrimination, as witnessed in the struggle against apartheid in South Africa. There is individual freedom which is lost, for example, when people are taken hostage. All these are great freedoms, worth fighting for and in some cases worth dying for.

But there is an even greater freedom, one worth giving everything for. The freedom which Jesus speaks of here is the highest and purest form and it is independent and different from all the others. On the one hand you can have none of the freedoms listed above and still be free. In the last 2,000 years men and women have willingly given up all of these "outward" freedoms because they wanted to attain something better. On the other hand you can have all the other freedoms and still not be free. The freedom Jesus offers is a personal and inner freedom of the soul. It is vital for us all. What does it mean?

1. Freedom of the heart (vs. 36)

Jesus points out that sin leads to slavery (vs. 34). Sin is self-centered. It involves self-assertion, pride, and arrogance. It can involve selfish ambition: the lust for power, money, and glory. It sometimes leads to selfish indulgence including drugs, alcoholism, or sexual immorality. All this makes us "a slave to sin."

But Jesus promises that "if the Son sets you free, you will be free indeed" (vs. 36).

Freedom from guilt

Guilt destroys. The only place to get rid of guilt is at the cross.

Freedom from addictive power

Addiction destroys but Jesus sets us free. We are not necessarily set free from temptation, but we are free from the addictive power of sin.

Freedom from death

The wages of sin is death (Romans 6:23). Jesus sets us free to look death in the face (Hebrews 2:14-15). He gives us eternal life (John 17:3).

Charles Kingsley said that there are two freedoms. First, there is false freedom, where a person is free to do what they like. Second, there is true freedom, where a person is free to do what they ought. Jesus sets us free to be our true selves as God intended us to be. He sets us free to love God, to love our neighbor as ourselves, and even to love ourselves in the sense of accepting ourselves as we are.

2. Freedom of the mind (vs. 32)

Christians are sometimes accused of being "narrow-minded" or "anti-intellectual"—as contrasted with "free thinking." Jesus says here that the opposite is true. Following Jesus is the way of intellectual freedom and integrity. The "truth" (vs. 32) is what has been revealed by God. Jesus is the truth (John 14:6), God's ultimate revelation. Knowing "the truth" is not about assenting to philosophical principles but about knowing a person. Knowing God and Jesus broadens our minds, gives us depth of insight, and scope of understanding. It does not provide all the answers, but gives us a true and reliable framework of thinking, a firm basis which allows us to explore life in all its fullness.

There is no greater freedom than the one Jesus offers. So let us fight for all the freedoms but let us first make sure that we have the freedom that Jesus alone gives.

Read again verse 32: "Then you will know the truth, and the truth will set you free." This is a great verse to learn by heart. We find freedom in knowing Jesus Christ: developing a relationship with God through prayer, reading the Bible, obeying Him, and serving Him. It is as we submit completely to God that we encounter true freedom.

Prayer:

Thank God for all the freedoms you are enjoying. In particular, thank Him for setting us free from guilt, addictive power, and death. Thank Him for setting us free to love God and our neighbor and to be our true selves as God intended us to be.

Wisdom Is Meaningless

¹²I, the Teacher, was king over Israel in Jerusalem. ¹³I devoted myself to study and to explore by wisdom all that is done under heaven. What a heavy burden God has laid on men! ¹⁴I have seen all the things that are done under the sun; all of them are meaningless, a chasing after the wind.

¹⁵What is twisted cannot be
    straightened;
  what is lacking cannot be counted.

¹⁶I thought to myself, "Look, I have grown and increased in wisdom more than anyone who has ruled over Jerusalem before me; I have experienced much of wisdom and knowledge." ¹⁷Then I applied myself to the understanding of wisdom, and also of madness and folly, but I learned that this, too, is a chasing after the wind.

¹⁸For with much wisdom comes much
    sorrow;
  the more knowledge, the more
    grief.

Pleasures Are Meaningless

2 I thought in my heart, "Come now, I will test you with pleasure to find out what is good." But that also proved to be meaningless. ²"Laughter," I said, "is foolish. And what does pleasure accomplish?" ³I tried cheering myself with wine, and embracing folly—my mind still guiding me with wisdom. I wanted to see what was worthwhile for men to do under heaven during the few days of their lives.

⁴I undertook great projects: I built houses for myself and planted vineyards. ⁵I made gardens and parks and planted all kinds of fruit trees in them. ⁶I made reservoirs to water groves of flourishing trees. ⁷I bought male and female slaves and had other slaves who were born in my house. I also owned more herds and flocks than anyone in Jerusalem before me. ⁸I amassed silver and gold for myself, and the treasure of kings and provinces. I acquired men and women singers, and a harem as well—the delights of the heart of man. ⁹I became greater by far than anyone in Jerusalem before me. In all this my wisdom stayed with me.

¹⁰I denied myself nothing my eyes
    desired;
  I refused my heart no pleasure.
My heart took delight in all my work,
    and this was the reward for all my
    labor.
¹¹Yet when I surveyed all that my hands
    had done
  and what I had toiled to achieve,
everything was meaningless, a
    chasing after the wind;
  nothing was gained under the
    sun.

Wisdom and Folly Are Meaningless
¹²Then I turned my thoughts to
    consider wisdom,
  and also madness and folly.
What more can the king's successor
    do
than what has already been done?
¹³I saw that wisdom is better than folly,
    just as light is better than darkness.
¹⁴The wise man has eyes in his head,
    while the fool walks in the darkness;
but I came to realize
    that the same fate overtakes them
    both.

¹⁵Then I thought in my heart,
"The fate of the fool will overtake
    me also.
What then do I gain by being wise?"
I said in my heart,
    "This too is meaningless."

Life's Great Riddle

"He's trying to find his way in a crazy world—just like we all are." This is how John McEnroe summed up the life of Bjorn Borg, five times Wimbledon tennis champion and McEnroe's former rival.

People are searching for meaning in life. Albert Camus, the French novelist, essayist and playwright said, "Man cannot live without meaning." The writer of Ecclesiastes, in the shoes of the great King Solomon, 3,000 years ago, speaks about the search for meaning without God. He looks at three secular philosophies which all have their modern equivalent.

1. Enlightenment (1:12-18)

He searches for "wisdom" and "knowledge." There is nothing wrong with this; indeed reason and science are vital and complementary to the Christian faith. But they only answer the "when?" and "how?" questions—not the "who?" and "why?" To seek knowledge apart from God can only be a "chasing after the wind."

True wisdom is found in a relationship with God through Jesus Christ. The apostle Paul tells us that in Him "are hidden all the treasures of wisdom and knowledge" (Colossians 2:3).

2. Enjoyment (2:1-3, 8, 10)

Hedonism is the doctrine that pleasure is the proper and best end of human beings. It can be a form of escapism. The writer tries laughter (vs. 2). There is nothing wrong with that, but it does not provide meaning. He tries stimulants (vs. 3). Many try to escape through drink or drugs. Then he tries music (vs. 8). Then sexual pleasure (vs. 8b). In fact Solomon had 700 wives and 300 mistresses! Yet all of this still did not satisfy (vs. 11).

"Innocent pleasures in moderation can provide relaxation for the body and mind and can foster family and other relationships. But pleasure, per se, offers no deep, lasting satisfaction or sense of fulfillment. The pleasure-centered person, too soon bored with each succeeding level of 'fun,' constantly cries for more and more. So the next new pleasure has to be bigger and better, more exciting, with a bigger 'high.' A person in this state becomes almost entirely narcissistic, interpreting all of life in terms of the pleasure it provides to the self here and now" (Stephen Covey, *Seven*

Habits of Highly Effective People, p. 115). The more you seek it, the less you find it. True joy and pleasure are found in a relationship with God. As the psalmist writes:

"You will fill me with joy in your presence, with eternal pleasures at your right hand" (Psalm 16:11b).

3. Enrichment (2:4-11)

Materialism is a tendency to prefer material possessions to spiritual values. In his search for meaning the writer tries building projects (vs. 4); houses (vss. 4-5); having a large staff (vs. 7); possessions (vs. 7b); money (vs. 8); greatness, success, and fame (vs. 9); work and career (vs. 10b). Yet none of this satisfies (see Ecclesiastes. 5:10-11).

Enrichment is to be found not in materialism but in Christ. The apostle Paul discovered for himself that everything else was "rubbish" compared to Christ. He wrote, "Whatever was to my profit I now consider loss for the sake of Christ. What is more, I consider everything a loss compared to the surpassing greatness of knowing Christ Jesus my Lord, for whose sake I have lost all things. I consider them rubbish, that I may gain Christ" (Philippians 3:7-8).

Ecclesiastes raises questions which the New Testament answers. Meaning is to be found not "under the sun" but "in the Son." If we seek enlightenment, enjoyment, and enrichment for and by themselves, they will be as elusive as the wind. We will never find them. But if we seek God, we will find them all. Jesus said, "Seek first his kingdom and his righteousness, and all these things will be given to you as well" (Matthew 6:33).

What are your goals in life? Why not decide today to make your first ambition "his kingdom and his righteousness"? Then you will find true wisdom, solid joy, and lasting riches.

Prayer:

O most merciful redeemer, friend and brother, may we know You more clearly, love You more dearly, and follow You more nearly, day by day. (Richard of Chichester 1197-1253)

⁸" 'I brought you to the land of the Amorites who lived east of the Jordan. They fought against you, but I gave them into your hands. I destroyed them from before you, and you took possession of their land. ⁹When Balak son of Zippor, the king of Moab, prepared to fight against Israel, he sent for Balaam son of Beor to put a curse on you. ¹⁰But I would not listen to Balaam, so he blessed you again and again, and I delivered you out of his hand.

¹¹" 'Then you crossed the Jordan and came to Jericho. The citizens of Jericho fought against you, as did also the Amorites, Perizzites, Canaanites, Hittites, Girgashites, Hivites and Jebusites, but I gave them into your hands. ¹²I sent the hornet ahead of you, which drove them out before you—also the two Amorite kings. You did not do it with your own sword and bow. ¹³So I gave you a land on which you did not toil and cities you did not build; and you live in them and eat from vineyards and olive groves that you did not plant.'

¹⁴"Now fear the LORD and serve him with all faithfulness. Throw away the gods your forefathers worshiped beyond the River and in Egypt, and serve the LORD. ¹⁵But if serving the LORD seems undesirable to you, then choose for yourselves this day whom you will serve, whether the gods your forefathers served beyond the River, or the gods of the Amorites, in whose land you are living. But as for me and my household, we will serve the LORD."

¹⁶Then the people answered, "Far be it from us to forsake the LORD to serve other gods! ¹⁷It was the LORD our God himself who brought us and our fathers up out of Egypt, from that land of slavery, and performed those great signs before our eyes. He protected us on our entire journey and among all the nations through which we traveled. ¹⁸And the LORD drove out before us all the nations, including the Amorites, who lived in the land. We too will serve the LORD, because he is our God."

¹⁹Joshua said to the people, "You are not able to serve the LORD. He is a holy God; he is a jealous God. He will not forgive your rebellion and your sins. ²⁰If you forsake the LORD and serve foreign gods, he will turn and bring disaster on you and make an end of you, after he has been good to you."

²¹ But the people said to Joshua, "No! We will serve the LORD."

²²Then Joshua said, "You are witnesses against yourselves that you have chosen to serve the LORD."

"Yes, we are witnesses," they replied.

²³"Now then," said Joshua, "throw away the foreign gods that are among you and yield your hearts to the LORD, the God of Israel."

²⁴And the people said to Joshua, "We will serve the LORD our God and obey him."

²⁵On that day Joshua made a covenant for the people, and there at Shechem he drew up for them decrees and laws. ²⁶And Joshua recorded these things in the Book of the Law of God. Then he took a large stone and set it up there under the oak near the holy place of the LORD.

²⁷"See!" he said to all the people. "This stone will be a witness against us. It has heard all the words the LORD has said to us. It will be a witness against you if you are untrue to your God."

Buried in the Promised Land
²⁸Then Joshua sent the people away, each to his own inheritance.

²⁹After these things, Joshua son of Nun, the servant of the LORD, died at the age of a hundred and ten. ³⁰And they buried him in the land of his inheritance, at Timnath Serah in the hill country of Ephraim, north of Mount Gaash.

What Shall I Choose to Live For?

Life is full of choices. What we choose to live for is the most important choice of all. It faces every human being and affects every aspect of our life. Once we have made this choice, it will help us to make every other choice in life.

Joshua, Moses' successor as leader of the Israelites, at the end of his life, summons all the people with him and tells them they have to choose how to spend the rest of their lives. He says, "choose for yourselves this day whom you will serve" (vs. 15).

1. Why do we have to choose?

Everyone is a servant—either voluntarily or involuntarily. Some people say, "I am free. I don't serve anyone." But that really is not an option. We either serve "the Lord" or "foreign gods." The gods referred to claimed to be modern and scientific with control over agriculture, sex, and fertility. "Other gods" in our context are any activities, habits, or attitudes that lead us away from the Lord, such as materialism, promiscuity, or self-centeredness. Serving other gods leads eventually to emptiness, guilt, and death. It reduces our ability to control our own lives, the very opposite of what it promises. Serving the Lord leads to freedom and the ability to make the right decisions for ourselves and our families.

2. Why should we choose the Lord?

Joshua's answer is that they should choose God because of what He has done for them: His call, gifts, deliverance, defeat of their enemies, and the promises He has fulfilled (vss. 17-18). From our perspective, God has sent His Son Jesus to die for us and His Spirit to come and give us new life. He has liberated us from guilt, addiction, fear, and death. He has set us free to know God, to love, and to be transformed into His likeness.

3. What does it mean to choose to serve Him?

Joshua says they must "serve him with all faithfulness" (vs. 14). Literally the word means "fullness," "completeness," "integrity." These people thought they could serve the Lord and keep the other gods as well. But serving the Lord involves all of our hearts and all of our lives.

4. How do we choose to serve Him?

Joshua's answer (vs. 23) is two-fold:

"throw away the foreign gods"

Make sure that God has no rivals for His affection. In the words of Dag Hammarskjold, "You cannot play with the animal in you without becoming wholly animal, play with falsehood without forfeiting your right to truth, play with cruelty without losing your sensitivity of mind. He who wants to keep his garden tidy doesn't reserve a plot of weeds."

" How about one day on, one day off sort of thing

"yield your hearts to the Lord"

We need to put every area of our lives into the hands of the Lord: our family, friends, time, work, money, sexuality, possessions, and abilities.

In Joshua 1:1, Moses is described as a "servant of the LORD" and Joshua as his assistant. In Joshua 24:29, Joshua is described as "the servant of the LORD." The apostle Paul was proud to describe himself as "a servant of Jesus Christ." Jesus saw Himself as "the suffering servant" of Isaiah 53. To be a servant of God is the highest calling a person can ever receive. Each of us can have this title—"servant of the Lord"—if we choose to go on serving Him throughout our lives.

Prayer:

Why not ask God to reveal if there are any "other gods" in your life? If there are, you could resolve today to get rid of them. Choose today to serve the Lord for the rest of your life. You will never regret it.

Bible Passage
1 Peter 1:3-9

1 Peter, an apostle of Jesus Christ,

To God's elect, strangers in the world, scattered throughout Pontus, Galatia, Cappadocia, Asia and Bithynia, ²who have been chosen according to the foreknowledge of God the Father, through the sanctifying work of the Spirit, for obedience to Jesus Christ and sprinkling by his blood:

Grace and peace be yours in abundance.

Praise to God for a Living Hope
³Praise be to the God and Father of our Lord Jesus Christ! In his great mercy he has given us new birth into a living hope through the resurrection of Jesus Christ from the dead, ⁴and into an inheritance that can never perish, spoil or fade—kept in heaven for you, ⁵who through faith are shielded by God's power until the coming of the salvation that is ready to be revealed in the last time. ⁶In this you greatly rejoice, though now for a little while you may have had to suffer grief in all kinds of trials. ⁷These have come so that your faith—of greater worth than gold, which perishes even though refined by fire—may be proved genuine and may result in praise, glory and honor when Jesus Christ is revealed. ⁸Though you have not seen him, you love him; and even though you do not see him now, you believe in him and are filled with an inexpressible and glorious joy, ⁹for you are receiving the goal of your faith, the salvation of your souls.

¹⁰Concerning this salvation, the prophets, who spoke of the grace that was to come to you, searched intently and with the greatest care, ¹¹trying to find out the time and circumstances to which the Spirit of Christ in them was pointing when he predicted the sufferings of Christ and the glories that would follow. ¹²It was revealed to them that they were not serving themselves but you, when they spoke of the things that have now been told you by those who have preached the gospel to you by the Holy Spirit sent from heaven. Even angels long to look into these things.

Be Holy
¹³Therefore, prepare your minds for action; be self-controlled; set your hope fully on the grace to be given you when Jesus Christ is revealed. ¹⁴As obedient children, do not conform to the evil desires you had when you lived in ignorance. ¹⁵But just as he who called you is holy, so be holy in all you do; ¹⁶for it is written: "Be holy, because I am holy."

¹⁷Since you call on a Father who judges each man's work impartially, live your lives as strangers here in reverent fear. ¹⁸For you know that it was not with perishable things such as silver or gold that you were redeemed from the empty way of life handed down to you from your forefathers, ¹⁹but with the precious blood of Christ, a lamb without blemish or defect. ²⁰He was chosen before the creation of the world, but was revealed in these last times for your sake. ²¹Through him you believe in God, who raised him from the dead and glorified him, and so your faith and hope are in God.

²²Now that you have purified yourselves by obeying the truth so that you have sincere love for your brothers, love one another deeply, from the heart. ²³For you have been born again, not of perishable seed, but of imperishable, through the living and enduring word of God. ²⁴For,

"All men are like grass,
  and all their glory is like the flowers
  of the field;
the grass withers and the flowers fall,
  ²⁵but the word of the Lord stands
  forever."

And this is the word that was preached to you.

The Pursuit of Happiness

All of us want to be happy. Peter tells us here how to find true happiness, how to be "filled with an inexpressible and glorious joy" (vs. 8). What causes happiness? How can we find this joy?

In David Myers' book, The Pursuit of Happiness, *he concludes that happy people have three things: 1) an optimistic outlook; 2) high self-esteem; and 3) close relationships.*

Where do we find these? The Apostle Peter tells us in this passage.

1. An optimistic outlook (vss. 3-5)

What does the future hold for us? Peter praises God for the possibility of "new birth" into a "living hope" (vs. 3). Biblical hope is not hazy but certain, growing in strength year by year.

When we "hope it'll be a nice day," we have no idea if it will be or not. However, when the Bible speaks of hope, it speaks of certainty because this hope is based on the resurrection of Jesus Christ, which really did happen. In a real place in Palestine, there is a real grave which is empty forever. Jesus Christ conquered death and is alive for eternity. Those who are born again through faith in Jesus Christ will do the same. Our future is entirely secure: we are "shielded by God's power for eternity" (vs. 5). This is a hope that far exceeds the hopes of this world.

Our inheritance is "ready to be revealed." We are like children waiting for our Christmas present without knowing exactly when Christmas will come. Normally we receive an inheritance when someone else dies, and when we die we leave one. But this inheritance we receive in full when we die. It will "never spoil" whereas everything we see around us here on earth will eventually perish. Our possessions here fade, but this inheritance will never fade. It is "kept in heaven" for us (vs. 4).

Our heavenly inheritance is "stored up" for us, reserved in our name (vs. 5) and guaranteed. God is watching over us, as He will do forever.

2. High self-esteem (vss.6-7)

The Old Testament prophesied that we would "walk with heads held high" (Leviticus 26:13). How is this possible? First, because we are forgiven by "His great mercy" (vs. 3). Life is not always easy. We may have to go through "various trials" (vs. 6) but Peter writes that within and beyond the pain and suffering, there is cause for rejoicing.

Why? First, because of the relative brevity of our trials in contrast with eternity: only "a little while" (vs. 6)—just like the pains of childbirth. Second, the results of the trials are that our faith is refined (vs. 7) (as gold is refined by fire) and proved to be genuine, which ultimately will result in "praise, glory and honor." This refers to our praise and worship of God, but here it may also mean that God will give praise to His servants (see Matthew 25:14-30).

3. Close relationships (vss.8-9)

At the core of our being there is a powerful longing for love and relationship. Pop star Geri Halliwell has spoken often of her burning desire for fame which, once fulfilled, turned into the terrible fear of losing it. Now despite her fame and success, she says, (speaking for many): "I just want to be happy… Yet, I feel really lonely. I want love in my life."

The Apostle Peter had seen Jesus. His listeners had not. They believed without having seen Him, but they longed to see Him and know Him.

Larry King is the CNN Talk show host who has interviewed many of the richest, most famous, most influential people in the world. He said this: "Jesus Christ had a more profound effect on mankind than any individual ever born. If there is one person in history I would like to interview, it would be Jesus."

Maybe we feel the same. We would love to ask Him all our unanswered questions. We can. We can know Him now and love Him now. The word used for love here implies a continual regular activity—a personal daily relationship with the ascended Lord Jesus. A personal trust in Christ and love for Him is the reason for our greatest joy. This surely is the secret of happiness. This is the ultimate close relationship. The other two headings stem from it.

We can thank God today for the inheritance waiting in heaven for us to enjoy forever. This will help get our current problems and anxieties in perspective. If we are going through difficult times, we can pray that God will sustain us by His Spirit and use the experience to give us a deeper understanding of ourselves and of Himself.

Prayer:

Join with the Apostle Peter in praising the God and Father of our Lord Jesus Christ. Praise Him for His great mercy, for your new birth, for your hope, for the resurrection of Jesus, for God's power shielding you, and all the other blessings mentioned in this passage. Thank Him for His love for you and tell Him how much you love Him. Ask Him to fill you today with "an inexpressible and glorious joy," and pray for your friends, family, neighbors, and coworkers that they may come to know this love and joy in their own lives.

[15]But the gift is not like the trespass. For if the many died by the trespass of the one man, how much more did God's grace and the gift that came by the grace of the one man, Jesus Christ, overflow to the many! [16]Again, the gift of God is not like the result of the one man's sin: The judgment followed one sin and brought condemnation, but the gift followed many trespasses and brought justification. [17]For if, by the trespass of the one man, death reigned through that one man, how much more will those who receive God's abundant provision of grace and of the gift of righteousness reign in life through the one man, Jesus Christ.

[18]Consequently, just as the result of one trespass was condemnation for all men, so also the result of one act of righteousness was justification that brings life for all men. [19]For just as through the disobedience of the one man the many were made sinners, so also through the obedience of the one man the many will be made righteous.

[20]The law was added so that the trespass might increase. But where sin increased, grace increased all the more, [21]so that, just as sin reigned in death, so also grace might reign through righ-teousness to bring eternal life through Jesus Christ our Lord.

Dead to Sin, Alive in Christ

6What shall we say, then? Shall we go on sinning so that grace may increase? [2]By no means! We died to sin; how can we live in it any longer? [3]Or don't you know that all of us who were baptized into Christ Jesus were baptized into his death? [4]We were therefore buried with him through baptism into death in order that, just as Christ was raised from the dead through the glory of the Father, we too may live a new life.

[5]If we have been united with him like this in his death, we will certainly also be united with him in his resurrection. [6]For we know that our old self was crucified with him so that the body of sin might be done away with, that we should no longer be slaves to sin—[7]because anyone who has died has been freed from sin.

[8]Now if we died with Christ, we believe that we will also live with him. [9]For we know that since Christ was raised from the dead, he cannot die again; death no longer has mastery over him. [10]The death he died, he died to sin once for all; but the life he lives, he lives to God.

[11]In the same way, count yourselves dead to sin but alive to God in Christ Jesus. [12]Therefore do not let sin reign in your mortal body so that you obey its evil desires. [13]Do not offer the parts of your body to sin, as instruments of wickedness, but rather offer yourselves to God, as those who have been brought from death to life; and offer the parts of your body to him as instruments of righteousness. [14]For sin shall not be your master, because you are not under law, but under grace.

Slaves to Righteousness

[15]What then? Shall we sin because we are not under law but under grace? By no means! [16]Don't you know that when you offer yourselves to someone to obey him as slaves, you are slaves to the one whom you obey—whether you are slaves to sin, which leads to death, or to obedience, which leads to righteousness? [17]But thanks be to God that, though you used to be slaves to sin, you wholeheartedly obeyed the form of teaching to which you were entrusted. [18]You have been set free from sin and have become slaves to righteousness.

[19]I put this in human terms because you are weak in your natural selves. Just as you used to offer the parts of your body in slavery to impurity and to ever-increasing wickedness, so now offer them in slavery to righteousness leading to holiness.

Freedom from Addiction

At 10:56 P.M. on the night of July 20, 1969 our world changed forever. Two American astronauts, Neil Armstrong and Buzz Aldrin, walked on the moon. One of the greatest events of the 20th century took place as the result of the lunar voyage of Apollo 11. To get there, the astronauts had to break out of the gravity pull of the earth. More energy was spent in the first few minutes of lift-off, in the first few miles of travel, than was used over the next days to travel half a million miles.

Habits and addictions have tremendous gravity pull. Breaking deeply imbedded habitual tendencies such as procrastination, impatience, a critical spirit, or selfishness involves more than a little willpower and a few minor changes in our lives. "Lift-off" takes a tremendous effort, but once we break out of the gravity pull, our freedom takes on a whole new dimension.

It is said that the only exercise some people get is jumping to the wrong conclusions. Having spoken in Romans 1—5 of forgiveness, justification by faith, and the righteousness of God (that it is possible to be put right with God however bad we have been), Paul now fears that some of his readers will jump to the wrong conclusion and say, "It does not matter if we continue to sin."

Some go on sinning voluntarily. Rasputin, the mad monk and evil genius, taught his followers to go and sin so that God could forgive and they could experience more of God's love. Others do so involuntarily. They have some habit they can't get rid of. It could be alcoholism, drugs, materialism, anger, bad temper, some sexual sin, kleptomania, greed, lying, or something else.

Whatever category we are in, the question is, "Shall we continue?" Paul's answer is, "By no means." This passage raises three vital questions.

1. What do we see when we look at the cross? (vss. 1-10)

Paul's argument is that we cannot continue to sin because we have died! Our baptism signifies the fact that when Jesus died on the cross, we died (vs. 3). When Jesus was buried, we were buried. When Jesus was raised, we were raised (vs. 4). Our old self has been crucified (vs. 6). Therefore, "we should no longer be slaves to sin" (vs. 6).

Bishop Taylor-Smith, former chaplain-general to the British armed forces, asked a young man, "When you think about the cross of Christ, what do you see?" He answered, "I see Christ and two thieves." The bishop asked, "What else do you see?" He replied, "I see the soldiers gambling . . . What are you fishing for?" The bishop replied, "If that is all you see, I think you will have trouble with the Christian life. When I see the cross, with all that, I see the old Bishop Taylor-Smith. I was crucified with Christ." Becoming a Christian involves a radical change. It is not a little addition. It is a new life.

2. What do you see when you look at yourself? (vs. 11)

Paul writes, "In the same way, count yourselves dead to sin but alive to God in Christ Jesus." This involves a radical new self-image. I died on February 16, 1974. My old self died and from then a new creation came into being, alive to God, and freed from the power of sin. We do not need to say, "I am an alcoholic because my father was" or, "I am bad-tempered because my mother was." We can be different. We need to see ourselves in a new way. We need a radical change in self-perception.

Augustine lived a wild and immoral life. At the age of 32 he was converted in answer to his mother's prayers. Shortly after his conversion he saw a woman he used to know. The moment he saw her he ran away. She called out, "Augustine! Don't you recognize me? It's me!" He replied, "I know it's you, but it's no longer me!"

3. How do we act on what we see? (vss. 12-13)

As the theologian Bishop Lesslie Newbigin wrote, "Everyone who has honestly faced the cross of Christ knows what is meant by this dying with Christ and knows that it is a reality, a deep and costly reality. And yet he knows also that the self which has died is still alive and has to be continually fought to the death. He knows that the new life in Christ which he has received is something which has to be daily put on again" (Lesslie Newbigin, *Household of God,* p. 119).

It is not instant holiness, but a lifelong process. We do not need to continue in addictive patterns of sin. Once we have seen the truth and believed it, we need to act on it. We will still be tempted. We need to resist, fight, refuse, stop it. We must not give in. We must surrender ourselves to God to be used for His purposes. Christians do sin. However, Jesus enables us to be forgiven and return to the right path. For we are no longer enslaved to sin but have been freed to live a brand-new life for God.

Prayer:

Look at the cross of Christ again today. Picture yourself dying with Christ, being buried, and rising with Him to a new life. See yourself as you are: a new creation, free from the ingrained patterns of the past. Ask for the Holy Spirit's help to live like the new person you truly are.

⁸By faith Abraham, when called to go to a place he would later receive as his inheritance, obeyed and went, even though he did not know where he was going. ⁹By faith he made his home in the promised land like a stranger in a foreign country; he lived in tents, as did Isaac and Jacob, who were heirs with him of the same promise. ¹⁰For he was looking forward to the city with foundations, whose architect and builder is God.

¹¹By faith Abraham, even though he was past age—and Sarah herself was barren—was enabled to become a father because he considered him faithful who had made the promise. ¹²And so from this one man, and he as good as dead, came descendants as numerous as the stars in the sky and as countless as the sand on the seashore.

¹³All these people were still living by faith when they died. They did not receive the things promised; they only saw them and welcomed them from a distance. And they admitted that they were aliens and strangers on earth. ¹⁴People who say such things show that they are looking for a country of their own. ¹⁵If they had been thinking of the country they had left, they would have had opportunity to return. ¹⁶Instead, they were longing for a better country—a heavenly one. Therefore God is not ashamed to be called their God, for he has prepared a city for them.

¹⁷By faith Abraham, when God tested him, offered Isaac as a sacrifice. He who had received the promises was about to sacrifice his one and only son, ¹⁸even though God had said to him, "It is through Isaac that your offspring will be reckoned." ¹⁹Abraham reasoned that God could raise the dead, and figuratively speaking, he did receive Isaac back from death.

²⁰By faith Isaac blessed Jacob and Esau in regard to their future.

²¹By faith Jacob, when he was dying, blessed each of Joseph's sons, and worshiped as he leaned on the top of his staff. ²²By faith Joseph, when his end was near, spoke about the exodus of the Israelites from Egypt and gave instructions about his bones.

²³By faith Moses' parents hid him for three months after he was born, because they saw he was no ordinary child, and they were not afraid of the king's edict. ²⁴By faith Moses, when he had grown up, refused to be known as the son of Pharaoh's daughter. ²⁵He chose to be mistreated along with the people of God rather than to enjoy the pleasures of sin for a short time. ²⁶He regarded disgrace for the sake of Christ as of greater value than the treasures of Egypt, because he was looking ahead to his reward. ²⁷By faith he left Egypt, not fearing the king's anger; he persevered because he saw him who is invisible. ²⁸By faith he kept the Passover and the sprinkling of blood, so that the destroyer of the firstborn would not touch the firstborn of Israel.

²⁹By faith the people passed through the Red Sea as on dry land; but when the Egyptians tried to do so, they were drowned.

³⁰By faith the walls of Jericho fell, after the people had marched around them for seven days.

³¹By faith the prostitute Rahab, because she welcomed the spies, was not killed with those who were disobedient.

³²And what more shall I say? I do not have time to tell about Gideon, Barak, Samson, Jephthah, David, Samuel and the prophets, ³³who through faith conquered kingdoms, administered justice, and gained what was promised; who shut the mouths of lions, ³⁴quenched the fury of the flames, and escaped the edge of the sword; whose weakness was turned to strength; and who became powerful in battle and routed foreign armies. ³⁵Women received back their dead, raised to life again. Others were tortured and refused to be released, so that they might gain a better resurrection.

What Is Faith?

Who is the greatest person who has ever lived? Any Christian would reply, "Jesus Christ." If you had asked a Jew that question they would have replied, without doubt, "Moses." To the Jews, Moses was the supreme figure of history. He had rescued them from slavery and given them the law.

In this letter the writer found it necessary to prove to these Jewish Christians that Jesus was greater than Moses (Hebrews 3). Here he shows that Moses was and is preeminently a man of faith, high up on God's honors list, raised up by God at a time when God's people were in great need.

Faith describes our relationship with God, which at heart is one of trust. Relationships depend on trust. The novelist Graham Greene wrote, "It is impossible to go through life without trust—that would be to be imprisoned in the cell of one's own self." The writer here highlights three aspects of Moses' faith:

1. Faith as choice (vss. 23-26)

Moses had great advantages in life. He was physically good-looking (Exodus 2:2). He was brought up in the Egyptian royal household and received a first-class education and training. He had the prospect of inheriting the great wealth of Egypt and experiencing all the pleasures of a royal prince, including as many wives and mistresses as he chose. Jewish tradition suggests that he had the prospect of gaining the throne itself, probably the most powerful throne of the time.

But Moses had another great advantage: the faith of his parents (vs. 23). He himself needed to make a choice. On the one hand, there was all that the world offered: money, sex, and power. On the other, he could identify with God's people, a slave nation despised by well-educated

Egyptians. Identifying with them meant danger, scorn, and suffering. As he looked at this second alternative he saw something of "greater value than the treasures of Egypt" (vs. 26): the reward that God offers. He saw that whereas the pleasures of this world are fleeting (vs. 25), God offers a lasting reward. Weighing the issues of time in the balance of eternity, he did what was absurd without God but wise with Him.

He decided to throw his weight in with God's people. He chose to follow the Lord. It involved Moses trusting the Lord enough to say (in the terms of the schoolchild mnemonic of faith) "**F**orsaking **A**ll, **I** **T**ake **H**im." This is the justifying FAITH of the New Testament.

2. Faith as perseverance (vs. 27)

Twice Moses left Egypt. He left first as a criminal on the run after killing an Egyptian. The second time, he left as leader of the people of God. In between he persevered, showing courage, determination, and endurance. Between the moment of choice and the moment of triumph there were many battles, but he trusted God throughout. Another schoolchild mnemonic for faith is, "**F**eeling **A**fraid, **I** **T**rust **H**im." He trusted the invisible God before the very visible Pharaoh. Faith is persevering and trusting in "him who is invisible" (vs. 27).

3. Faith requires expectancy (vss. 28-29)

Moses did what God told him to do. He had a conviction of God's power to kill and a belief that He would do what He had said. He believed that God could perform signs and wonders, the greatest of which was crossing the Red Sea (vs. 29). Again faith involves trust. Perhaps this is the "gift of faith" which Paul speaks about (1 Corinthians 12:9), described by Professor Dunn as "that mysterious 'surge of confidence' which sometimes arises within a person in a particular situation" (J. Dunn, *Jesus and the Spirit*, p. 211).

Our own faith begins with a choice, and often that choice involves giving things up. Then we need to stick to it, believing in God's power to work in our lives. There will be times when God gives us a special "gift of faith"—a mysterious surge of confidence.

Prayer:

Thank God today for the example of Moses and pray that by the help of God's Holy Spirit you will be enabled to make the right choices, that you will persevere in your faith, and that God will give you the "gift of faith."

You might like to pray the prayer that Mother Theresa used to pray.

"Lord, increase my faith, bless my efforts and work, now and forever-more, Amen."

Bible Passage
Mark 4:1-20

[33]"Who are my mother and my brothers?" he asked.

[34]Then he looked at those seated in a circle around him and said, "Here are my mother and my brothers! [35]Whoever does God's will is my brother and sister and mother."

The Parable of the Sower

4 Again Jesus began to teach by the lake. The crowd that gathered around him was so large that he got into a boat and sat in it out on the lake, while all the people were along the shore at the water's edge. [2]He taught them many things by parables, and in his teaching said: [3]"Listen! A farmer went out to sow his seed. [4]As he was scattering the seed, some fell along the path, and the birds came and ate it up. [5]Some fell on rocky places, where it did not have much soil. It sprang up quickly, because the soil was shallow. [6]But when the sun came up, the plants were scorched, and they withered because they had no root. [7]Other seed fell among thorns, which grew up and choked the plants, so that they did not bear grain. [8]Still other seed fell on good soil. It came up, grew and produced a crop, multiplying thirty, sixty, or even a hundred times."

[9]Then Jesus said, "He who has ears to hear, let him hear."

[10]When he was alone, the Twelve and the others around him asked him about the parables. [11]He told them, "The secret of the kingdom of God has been given to you. But to those on the outside everything is said in parables [12]so that,

" 'they may be ever seeing but
never perceiving,
and ever hearing but never
understanding;
otherwise they might turn and be
forgiven!' "

[13]Then Jesus said to them, "Don't you understand this parable? How then will you understand any parable? [14]The farmer sows the word. [15]Some people are like seed along the path, where the word is sown. As soon as they hear it, Satan comes and takes away the word that was sown in them. [16]Others, like seed sown on rocky places, hear the word and at once receive it with joy. [17]But since they have no root, they last only a short time. When trouble or persecution comes because of the word, they quickly fall away. [18]Still others, like seed sown among thorns, hear the word; [19]but the worries of this life, the deceitfulness of wealth and the desires for other things come in and choke the word, making it unfruitful. [20]Others, like seed sown on good soil, hear the word, accept it, and produce a crop—thirty, sixty or even a hundred times what was sown."

A Lamp on a Stand

[21]He said to them, "Do you bring in a lamp to put it under a bowl or a bed? Instead, don't you put it on its stand? [22]For whatever is hidden is meant to be disclosed, and whatever is concealed is meant to be brought out into the open. [23]If anyone has ears to hear, let him hear."

[24]"Consider carefully what you hear," he continued. "With the measure you use, it will be measured to you—and even more. [25]Whoever has will be given more; whoever does not have, even what he has will be taken from him."

The Parable of the Growing Seed

[26]He also said, "This is what the kingdom of God is like. A man scatters seed on the ground. [27]Night and day, whether he sleeps or gets up, the seed sprouts and grows, though he does not know how. [28]All by itself the soil produces grain—first the stalk, then the head, then the full kernel in the head. [29]As soon as the grain is ripe, he puts the sickle to it, because the harvest has come."

How to Maximize Your Potential

Jesus often told stories to get people thinking. In this case, because the disciples didn't seem to understand the story, He explained it to them in detail. He said that the seed was the Word of God and that the different soils represented different people. This parable may apply to all of us at different times in our lives.

There are four types of response to Jesus' message.

1. The hard-hearted (vss. 4, 15)

Some seed "fell along the path" and "the birds came and ate it up" (vs. 4). Jesus explains that this represents people who hear the Word but "Satan comes and takes away the word that was sown in them" (vs. 15). This is when we hear the Word of God but it makes no deep impression. We do nothing about it. There are those who shrug off any mention of Christ with complete lack of interest. In effect, the devil has come and taken away the message.

2. The faint-hearted (vss. 5-6, 16-17)

The seed lands on rocky ground with little soil and therefore the plant does not take root properly (vss. 5-6). The intense heat of the sun kills off the plant. Jesus explains that this soil represents those people who when they hear the Word of God "receive it with joy. But since they have no root, they last only a short time. When trouble or persecution comes because of the word, they quickly fall away" (vss. 16-17). When something goes wrong in our life or we suffer ridicule or opposition, our enthusiasm for God fades because there is no root. The root is the part of our lives which no one sees: our secret life with God which gives strength to what appears above the surface.

3. The half-hearted (vss. 7, 18-19)

Here the thorns grow faster than the wheat and therefore choke it (vs. 7). Jesus said these thorns are first "the worries of this life." These could be job pressures, financial worries, or concerns about one's family or even ministry. Secondly, the thorns are "the deceitfulness of wealth," perhaps the desire for promotion at work, the grip of financial success, or the blinding goal of becoming rich. Thirdly, the thorns are "the desires for other things" which can creep in and "choke the word, making it unfruitful." These things could be good in themselves (making a home, doing our job well, caring for children, keeping fit, putting time and energy into a relationship, and so on), but if they distract us from following Christ we will be unfruitful.

4. The whole-hearted (vss. 8, 20)

The seed that falls on the good soil produces fruit thirty-fold, sixty-fold or even a hundred times what was sown (vss. 8, 20). The minimum is thirty times but they all had a very high output. These are the Christians who persevere and do not lose heart. We may feel that we have little to offer but the issue is not how much we have but what we do with what we have. If we hear God's Word and respond to it throughout our lives we will produce a massive crop.

For most of us there have been times when we have not been whole-hearted. This does not mean that we have to remain like that. We can repent of the times we have not responded to God, or when difficulties or opposition have overcome us, or "other things" have distracted us from following Christ.

What matters now is that we make the most of the rest of our lives—that we maximize our potential fruitfulness. We do this by constantly allowing the Word of God to penetrate deeply into our lives—allowing Him to speak to us through the Bible, as we pray, and through others in the Christian community.

Determine not to allow the difficulties or opposition to put you off. Beware of the "other things" that can so easily creep in. Resolve to respond wholeheartedly to God's Word, with the help of His Holy Spirit, throughout your life.

Prayer:

Commit yourself—heart, mind, and body—everything you have to the Lord. Give yourself to Him and ask Him to give you the ability to hear His word, accept it, and produce a crop throughout the rest of your life.

Bible Passage
James 4:1-12

⁷All kinds of animals, birds, reptiles and creatures of the sea are being tamed and have been tamed by man, ⁸but no man can tame the tongue. It is a restless evil, full of deadly poison.

⁹With the tongue we praise our Lord and Father, and with it we curse men, who have been made in God's likeness. ¹⁰Out of the same mouth come praise and cursing. My brothers, this should not be. ¹¹Can both fresh water and salt water flow from the same spring? ¹²My brothers, can a fig tree bear olives, or a grapevine bear figs? Neither can a salt spring produce fresh water.

Two Kinds of Wisdom

¹³Who is wise and understanding among you? Let him show it by his good life, by deeds done in the humility that comes from wisdom. ¹⁴But if you harbor bitter envy and selfish ambition in your hearts, do not boast about it or deny the truth. ¹⁵Such "wisdom" does not come down from heaven but is earthly, unspiritual, of the devil. ¹⁶For where you have envy and selfish ambition, there you find disorder and every evil practice.

¹⁷But the wisdom that comes from heaven is first of all pure; then peace-loving, considerate, submissive, full of mercy and good fruit, impartial and sincere. ¹⁸Peacemakers who sow in peace raise a harvest of righteousness.

Submit Yourselves to God

4 What causes fights and quarrels among you? Don't they come from your desires that battle within you? ²You want something but don't get it. You kill and covet, but you cannot have what you want. You quarrel and fight. You do not have, because you do not ask God. ³When you ask, you do not receive, because you ask with wrong motives, that you may spend what you get on your pleasures.

⁴You adulterous people, don't you know that friendship with the world is hatred toward God? Anyone who chooses to be a friend of the world becomes an enemy of God. ⁵Or do you think Scripture says without reason that the spirit he caused to live in us envies intensely? ⁶But he gives us more grace. That is why Scripture says:

"God opposes the proud
but gives grace to the humble."

⁷Submit yourselves, then, to God. Resist the devil, and he will flee from you. ⁸Come near to God and he will come near to you. Wash your hands, you sinners, and purify your hearts, you double-minded. ⁹Grieve, mourn and wail. Change your laughter to mourning and your joy to gloom. ¹⁰Humble yourselves before the Lord, and he will lift you up.

¹¹Brothers, do not slander one another. Anyone who speaks against his brother or judges him speaks against the law and judges it. When you judge the law, you are not keeping it, but sitting in judgment on it. ¹²There is only one Lawgiver and Judge, the one who is able to save and destroy. But you—who are you to judge your neighbor?

Boasting About Tomorrow

¹³Now listen, you who say, "Today or tomorrow we will go to this or that city, spend a year there, carry on business and make money." ¹⁴Why, you do not even know what will happen tomorrow. What is your life? You are a mist that appears for a little while and then vanishes. ¹⁵Instead, you ought to say, "If it is the Lord's will, we will live and do this or that." ¹⁶As it is, you boast and brag. All such boasting is evil. ¹⁷Anyone, then, who knows the good he ought to do and doesn't do it, sins.

Right Relationships

James, the brother of Jesus, isolates three great problems facing the church and society. First, there is division—"fights and quarrels" (vss. 1-3). Secondly, there is the problem of dissatisfied lives (vs. 2). If we set our hearts on pleasure, as many do, we will never be satisfied. Thirdly, we suffer from a lack of spiritual power (vs. 3). How do we deal with these? The root of the problem is a breakdown of relationships. In this passage James urges us to get our relationships right.

1. Right relationship with God (vss. 4-6)

James sees the Christian's relationship with God as akin to marriage, so that "friendship with the world" (meaning the fallen world, organized in opposition to God) is the equivalent of adultery. The apostle John takes up this theme in 1 John 2, warning (in vs. 15), "Do not love the world or anything in the world." In the following verse, he expands his point. The true purpose of our life is not to satisfy ourselves physically or materially nor to seek our identity in so-called success and worldly position. Those who seek satisfaction in these areas will never be satisfied because only a friendship with God can satisfy. God hates to see us go after other things (vs. 5) and if we persist in doing so will oppose us (vs. 6). But if we humbly ask for His help He will give us His grace and His undeserved love. He is tirelessly on our side. God is so good that it is only reasonable to submit ourselves to Him (vs. 7). If we do so, we will desire what He desires and He will give us the desires of our hearts.

2. Right relationship with evil (vss. 7-10)

We are called to fight the devil tooth and nail. The devil is the ruler of the world apart from God and wants to draw us away from this love relationship with God. He tries to drag us away through addiction, bad temper, theft, lust, lying, unforgiveness, or some other sin. The battle is great but if we resist him, he flees (vs. 7). As we draw near to God, He draws near to us (vs. 8).

We are called to hate sin (vss. 8-9), to wash our hands and purify our hearts. We must put right what we do and what we think. We must not be "double-minded" but have to decide between God and the world. In verse 9, James is not condemning all laughter. Laughter is healing and relieves stress and tension but we must not use complacent laughter where our actions call for regret and repentance (vs. 9). As we humble ourselves He will lift us up (vs. 10).

3. Right relationships with each other (vss. 11-12)

When we get right with God we will also want to be at peace with our brothers and sisters. James says, "Do not slander one another" (vs. 11). Slander and back-biting are illustrations of a lack of humility. We bring others down in order to puff ourselves up.

Three times he speaks of our fellow Christians as brothers and neighbors. In speaking evil we are failing to love our brothers and neighbors. The law tells us to love one another. In speaking against one another, we are speaking against the law. In a negative and critical environment people shrivel up and die emotionally. The opposite is an atmosphere of love and encouragement which enables people to blossom. We demonstrate our love for God by the way we treat our brothers and neighbors.

Christianity for James, as for Jesus, is about relationships. It is about loving God and loving others. It is about resisting anything which gets in the way. If we get our relationships right, all the rest will follow. We will find ourselves totally aligned to the will of God. If we love God and love our neighbor there is nothing that God will not do for us.

"Resist the devil, and he will flee from you. Come near to God and he will come near to you" (James 4:7-8). It is worth learning this by heart, meditating on it and using it whenever we are tempted.

Prayer:

Ask God for the strength to resist temptation—"lead us not into temptation but deliver us from evil"—and pray that God will draw near to you as you draw near to Him.

Psalms

BOOK 1

Psalms 1–41

Psalm 1

¹Blessed is the man
  who does not walk in the coun-
sel
    of the wicked
or stand in the way of sinners
    or sit in the seat of mockers.
²But his delight is in the law of the
  LORD,
and on his law he meditates day
and
    night.
³He is like a tree planted by
streams
    of water,
  which yields its fruit in season
and whose leaf does not wither.
    Whatever he does prospers.
⁴Not so the wicked!
  They are like chaff
  that the wind blows away.
⁵Therefore the wicked will not
stand
    in the judgment,
  nor sinners in the assembly of
the
    righteous.
⁶For the LORD watches over the
way
    of the righteous,
  but the way of the wicked
  will perish.

Psalm 2

¹Why do the nations conspire
  and the peoples plot in vain?
²The kings of the earth take their stand
  and the rulers gather together
against the LORD
  and against his Anointed One.
³"Let us break their chains," they say,
  and throw off their fetters."
⁴The One enthroned in heaven laughs;
  the Lord scoffs at them.
⁵Then he rebukes them in his anger
  and terrifies them in his wrath,
    saying,
⁶"I have installed my King
  on Zion, my holy hill."
⁷I will proclaim the decree of the LORD:
He said to me, "You are my Son ;
  today I have become your Father.
⁸Ask of me,
  and I will make the nations your
    inheritance,
  the ends of the earth your
    possession.
⁹You will rule them with an iron
    scepter ;
you will dash them to pieces like
    pottery."
¹⁰Therefore, you kings, be wise;
  be warned, you rulers of the earth.
¹¹Serve the LORD with fear
  and rejoice with trembling.
¹²Kiss the Son, lest he be angry
  and you be destroyed in your way,
for his wrath can flare up in a moment.
  Blessed are all who take refuge in
    him.

How Can the Bible Become a Delight?

Marion was studying English at university. In the second term she had to write an essay on a particular modern writer. She found his work boring: she could not get into his novels or short stories and the deadline for her essay loomed closer and closer with very little achieved.

Glad to have the chance to get away from her largely fruitless studies, she went with some of her friends to a party at their teacher's home. During the evening her teacher introduced her to a very good-looking man in his early thirties.

He seemed to know a lot about literature and was extremely interesting. Marion was captivated by him. During the conversation, Marion discovered him to be the modern writer who was the subject of her essay. That night she went home and in the small hours started to read page after page of his work and found it absolutely fascinating. (Drive the Point Home, *Graham Twelftree, Monarch 1994, p.38.*)

Once we know the author of the Bible, it too can become an exciting book. The psalmist says that their "delight is in the law of the LORD" (vs. 2). All he had at this stage were the first five books of the Bible. They were his delight. He encourages us to do as he did—to meditate day and night (vs. 2)—which involves reading and thinking about the Bible regularly. Perhaps set aside a particular time each day to study God's Word.

The psalmist encourages us that if we delight in the law of the Lord in this way, then certain things will happen in our lives.

1. We shall produce fruit

He says, "They are like trees planted by streams of water, which yield their fruit in season" (vs. 3). This promise is that as we immerse ourselves in the Bible, our life will produce fruit, the fruit of the Spirit. Not only will our own life change but this fruit will include the transformation of other people's lives. It is not only for our benefit that we read the Bible but so that we can be a blessing to others: our friends, colleagues, neighbors, and the society in which we live. This is the fruit that will last into eternity (John 15:16).

2. We shall persevere

The second promise given to those whose delight is in the law of the Lord is that they will be like trees whose "leaf does not wither" (vs. 3). If we stay close to Jesus Christ through His Word, we will not dry up or lose our spiritual vitality. It is not enough to have great spiritual experiences, although they are very important and very wonderful. Unless we are deeply rooted in Jesus Christ, in His Word and in that relationship with Him, we won't be able to withstand the storms of life. If we are rooted in that relationship and delighting in His Word, then when the storms come we shall stand firm.

3. We will prosper

The psalmist says that the person who delights in the Word of God will prosper in "whatever he does" (vs. 3). Our lives may not be ones of material prosperity, but we shall prosper in the ways that really matter in life: in our relationship with God, our relationships with others, and the transforming of our characters into the likeness of Jesus Christ. These things are far more valuable than material wealth.

With the psalmist and millions of other Christians, why not determine to make the Bible your delight? Decide today to make reading the Bible a high priority in your life. Read it every day, if possible. The promise of Scripture is that if you delight in the law of the Lord you will become like a tree planted by streams of water, you will yield "fruit" in your life and you will prosper in whatever you do.

George Müller began a ministry that rescued hundreds of starving orphans from death in the slums of England. As important as his role was in showing these needy children the love of their heavenly Father, the ministry was never Müller's first priority. He believed God's highest call on his life was for intimate relationship with Him.

God had shown him that the way to have this was through daily Bible meditation. He said, "God showed me that I should go to His Word to chew on it early in the morning. This is not something I do for my ministry, but something for me personally, that I would be nourished." History testifies to the tremendous impact this meditation had on his life and ministry. Imagine what God could accomplish through each of us if we started each day by meditating on the Bible.

Prayer:

Thank God for the Bible and ask Him to speak to you each day as you read it. Pray along with the Psalmist, "Open my eyes that I may see wonderful things in your law" (Psalm 119:18).

Psalm 51

For the director of music. A psalm of David. When the prophet Nathan came to him after David had committed adultery with Bathsheba.

¹Have mercy on me, O God,
  according to your unfailing love;
according to your great compassion
  blot out my transgressions.
²Wash away all my iniquity
  and cleanse me from my sin.
³For I know my transgressions,
  and my sin is always before me.
⁴Against you, you only, have I sinned
  and done what is evil in your
sight, so that you are proved right
when you
    speak
  and justified when you judge.
⁵Surely I was sinful at birth,
  sinful from the time my mother
    conceived me.
⁶Surely you desire truth in the inner
    parts;
you teach me wisdom in the inmost
    place.
⁷Cleanse me with hyssop, and I will
be
    clean;
  wash me, and I will be whiter
than
    snow.
⁸Let me hear joy and gladness;
  let the bones you have crushed
    rejoice.
⁹Hide your face from my sins
  and blot out all my iniquity.
¹⁰Create in me a pure heart, O God,
  and renew a steadfast spirit within
    me.
¹¹Do not cast me from your presence
  or take your Holy Spirit from
me.
¹²Restore to me the joy of your
    salvation
  and grant me a willing spirit, to

sustain me.
¹³Then I will teach transgressors
your
    ways,
  and sinners will turn back to you.
¹⁴Save me from bloodguilt, O God,
  the God who saves me,
  and my tongue will sing of your
    righteousness.
¹⁵O Lord, open my lips,
  and my mouth will declare your
    praise.
¹⁶You do not delight in sacrifice, or I
    would bring it;
  you do not take pleasure in burnt
    offerings.
¹⁷The sacrifices of God are a broken
    spirit;
  a broken and contrite heart,
  O God, you will not despise.
¹⁸In your good pleasure make Zion
    prosper;
  build up the walls of Jerusalem.
¹⁹Then there will be righteous
    sacrifices,
  whole burnt offerings to delight
you;
  then bulls will be offered on your
    altar.

Psalm 52

For the director of music. A maskil of David. When Doeg the Edomite had gone to Saul and told him: "David has gone to the house of Ahimelech."

¹Why do you boast of evil, you mighty
    man?
  Why do you boast all day long,
  you who are a disgrace in the eyes
    of God?
²Your tongue plots destruction;
  it is like a sharpened razor,
  you who practice deceit.
³You love evil rather than good,
  falsehood rather than speaking the
    truth.   *Selah*

Dealing with Guilt

What do we do when we have sinned and let God down? How do we get ourselves right with God? How do we receive His mercy?

King David wrote this psalm when he was wracked by guilt after he had committed adultery with Bathsheba, then engineered the death of her husband and finally taken her to be his wife. All this was made public by the prophet Nathan, and the enormity of what he had done filled David with remorse (see 2 Samuel 11—12).

1. David saw the need for God's mercy (vss. 1-5)

We cannot appreciate the mercy of God until we see our own need and the seriousness of our sin. David uses three words to describe his own wrong-doing.

Transgression (vss. 1, 3)

This means crossing a boundary. God's boundaries are there for our protection, security, and enjoyment. When we cross them people get hurt. In one series of actions David had broken four commands. He was guilty of coveting, theft, adultery, and murder. One sin had led to another.

Sin (vs. 4)

This means missing the mark or falling short of a target. It is the difference between what we are and what we might have been. David recognizes that he has sinned against God. The essence of sin is revolt against God. He does not try to justify himself (vs. 4).

"*David murdered; I stole sweets. So there is a chance*"

Iniquity (vs. 5)

This points to the fact that our whole nature and character are flawed. Human nature is infected by sin. However, this is not incompatible with human responsibility. David accepts responsibility and does not make excuses for his actions. We cannot blame our parents, God, friends, or even the devil. A man of mature years at the height of his career with great power and popularity is prepared to admit he is a sinner in need of God's mercy.

2. David saw the greatness of God's mercy

He uses three expressions and three metaphors.

Library

He prays that God would "blot out" his transgressions (vs. 1). It is as if God has a book of guilt and will blot out the entries.

Laundry

The effect of sin is to make us dirty. David prays that God will wash him clean (vs. 2).

Leprosy

David prays that God would "cleanse (him) with hyssop" (vs. 7). This was how a leper was cleansed. A bunch of hyssop was used to sprinkle sacrificial blood onto him seven times. Just as the healing of leprosy involves creation of new skin, so David prays, "Create in me a pure heart, O God, and renew a steadfast spirit within me" (vs. 10).

Only in the light of the cross can this be fully understood. Our sins have been blotted out because Jesus paid the price for them. We "were washed . . . in the name of the Lord Jesus Christ and by the Spirit of our God" (1 Corinthians 6:11). The blood of Christ cleanses us from all sin (1 John 1:7, RSV).

3. David saw the results of God's mercy (vss. 11-19)

He did not escape all the tragic consequences of his sin (see 2 Samuel 12 and the rest of the history of Israel). However, David did recover much of what he had lost through his sin.

His sense of the presence of God (vs. 11)
The power of the Holy Spirit in his life (vs. 11)
The joy of his salvation (vs. 12)
His enthusiasm for doing God's work (vs. 12)

The effectiveness of his ministry (vs. 13)

His intimacy with God (vs. 15)

God in His mercy restored all this when David came and said, "Have mercy on me." God will never despise a "broken and contrite heart" (vs. 17). However serious our sin, God's mercy is even greater.

Prayer:

Ask God to reveal to you if there is anything for which you need to ask God's forgiveness and then read this psalm as your own prayer to God.

¹⁴Satisfy us in the morning with your
    unfailing love,
      that we may sing for joy and be glad
        all our days.
¹⁵Make us glad for as many days as you
    have afflicted us,
      for as many years as we have seen
        trouble.
¹⁶May your deeds be shown to your
    servants,
      your splendor to their children.
¹⁷May the favor of the Lord our God
    rest upon us;
      establish the work of our hands for
        us—
      yes, establish the work of our hands.

Psalm 91

¹He who dwells in the shelter of the
    Most High
    will rest in the shadow of the
      Almighty.
²I will say of the LORD, "He is my
    refuge and my fortress,
    my God, in whom I trust."
³Surely he will save you from the
    fowler's snare
    and from the deadly pestilence.
⁴He will cover you with his feathers,
    and under his wings you will find
      refuge;
    his faithfulness will be your shield
      and rampart.
⁵You will not fear the terror of night,
    nor the arrow that flies by day,
⁶nor the pestilence that stalks in the
    darkness,
    nor the plague that destroys at
      midday.
⁷A thousand may fall at your side,
    ten thousand at your right hand,
    but it will not come near you.
⁸You will only observe with your eyes

and see the punishment of the
    wicked.
⁹If you make the Most High your
    dwelling—
    even the LORD, who is my refuge—
¹⁰then no harm will befall you,
    no disaster will come near your tent.
¹¹For he will command his angels
    concerning you
    to guard you in all your ways;
¹²they will lift you up in their hands,
    so that you will not strike your foot
      against a stone.
¹³You will tread upon the lion and the
    cobra;
    you will trample the great lion and
      the serpent.
¹⁴"Because he loves me," says the
    LORD, "I will rescue him;
    I will protect him, for he
      acknowledges my name.
¹⁵He will call upon me, and I will
    answer him;
    I will be with him in trouble,
    I will deliver him and honor him.
¹⁶With long life will I satisfy him
    and show him my salvation."

Psalm 92

A psalm. A song. For the Sabbath day.

¹It is good to praise the LORD
    and make music to your name,
      O Most High,
²to proclaim your love in the morning
    and your faithfulness at night,
³to the music of the ten-stringed lyre
    and the melody of the harp.
⁴For you make me glad by your deeds,
    O LORD;
    I sing for joy at the works of your
      hands.

Overcoming Fear

A large and dangerous-looking 50-year-old truck driver was asked on a candid camera TV interview: "If you could be any age you wanted what age would you be?" There was a long silence and then he replied, "Three. When you are three you don't have any responsibilities." He was yearning for the feeling of childhood: the sense that you are loved, protected, and perfectly safe. This is the sense, above all, that somebody else is in charge.

The fears of life are many and varied: the future, the dark, being laughed at or attacked, fear of HIV, bankruptcy, loneliness, growing old, death, singleness, relationships breaking up, illness, failure, occult powers, war, and so on. However, the most common command in the Bible is, "Do not fear." It occurs 366 times in the Bible (one for each day and an extra one to cover leap years).

Here, the psalmist expresses one of the many moods of faith. He is celebrating his own confidence in the sheltering providence of God. Perhaps he had just been protected by God in a dangerous situation. All of us (just like those we read about in Scripture) are likely to experience such times of joy and celebration, as well as times of sadness and frustration. Throughout the ups and downs of life, we know that no final harm can touch us because nothing can ever separate us from the love of God in the present or throughout eternity (Romans 8:35-39).

With that knowledge, the psalmist encourages us to live lives free from fear, stating in verses 9-10: "If you make the Most High your dwelling . . . then no harm will befall you." He is, of course, not saying that everything will turn out just as we want it to. It does not mean that we can avoid times of trouble—see verse 15. Faith in the sheltering wings of God does not remove physical danger or the need for precaution against it. However, every Christian has the assurance that God is involved in every detail of our lives for all of eternity.

1. The psalmist testifies from his own experience (vss. 1-2)

Four names for God are given. He is "the Most High"—everything is under His control. He is "the Almighty"—the all-powerful one. He is "the LORD"—the universe is subject to His lordship. He is "my God"—He is in a personal relationship with those who follow Him.

There are four metaphors of security. We are safe in His "shelter," "shadow," "refuge," and "fortress." There are three positions of security: dwelling, abiding, and trusting.

2. The psalmist speaks to us (vss. 3-13)

In verses 3-6, he promises God's protection from every kind of danger, "the fowler's snare" and "the deadly pestilence" (vs. 3). Then he says that God is like an eagle protecting us under His wings, giving a picture of His tender love (vs. 4). His faithfulness is a "shield and rampart" (vs. 4), a picture of military protection. He promises release from the "terror of night" (vs. 5)—the sudden fears, often out of proportion, that prevent us from sleeping. He also promises protection from sudden attacks or disasters (vs. 6).

In verses 7-10, he promises God's individual protection from ultimate harm. If we love Him (vs. 14) nothing can take away our relationship with Him. God is sovereign and loving. As Paul puts it in the New Testament, "In all things God works for the good of those who love him, who have been called according to his purpose" (Romans 8:28).

In verses 11-13, he even promises miraculous protection saying that God promises that He will send His angels to look after us.

3. The Lord Himself speaks (vss. 14-16)

He promises eight wonderful things: deliverance, protection, answered prayer, His presence, rescue, honor, long life (now eternal life), and most important of all, salvation. He promises all of this to those who "love me" and who "acknowledge my name" and who "call upon me"—those who walk in an intimate relationship with God.

Today, bring all your fears and anxieties to God in prayer. As the apostle Peter wrote, "Cast all your anxiety on him because he cares for you" (1 Peter 5:7). It is not that we don't have any responsibilities nor that we can go through life without facing problems, difficulties, and sadness. But it is possible to enjoy the security of childhood forever. Someone else is in charge and whatever happens, we can be sure that we are loved, protected, and ultimately perfectly safe forever.

Prayer:

You might like to pray the prayer of St Augustine of Hippo (A.D. 354-430):

"O God, grant us in all our perplexities your guidance,
in all our dangers your protection,
and in all our sorrows your peace,
through Jesus Christ our Lord, Amen."

Bible Passage
Proverbs 16:1-9

²⁹The LORD is far from the wicked
but he hears the prayer of the
righteous.

³⁰A cheerful look brings joy to the
heart,
and good news gives health to the
bones.

³¹He who listens to a life-giving rebuke
will be at home among the wise.

³²He who ignores discipline despises
himself,
but whoever heeds correction gains
understanding.

³³The fear of the LORD teaches a man
wisdom,
and humility comes before honor.

16 To man belong the plans of the
heart,
but from the LORD comes the reply
of the tongue.

²All a man's ways seem innocent to
him,
but motives are weighed by the
LORD.

³Commit to the LORD whatever you do,
and your plans will succeed.

⁴The LORD works out everything for
his own ends—
even the wicked for a day of
disaster.

⁵The LORD detests all the proud of
heart.
Be sure of this: They will not go
unpunished.

⁶Through love and faithfulness sin is
atoned for;

through the fear of the LORD a man
avoids evil.

⁷When a man's ways are pleasing to
the LORD,
he makes even his enemies live at
peace with him.

⁸Better a little with righteousness
than much gain with injustice.

⁹In his heart a man plans his course,
but the LORD determines his steps.

¹⁰The lips of a king speak as an oracle,
and his mouth should not betray
justice.

¹¹Honest scales and balances are from
the LORD;
all the weights in the bag are of his
making.

¹²Kings detest wrongdoing,
for a throne is established through
righteousness.

¹³Kings take pleasure in honest lips;
they value a man who speaks the
truth.

¹⁴A king's wrath is a messenger of
death,
but a wise man will appease it.

¹⁵When a king's face brightens, it
means life;
his favor is like a rain cloud in
spring.

¹⁶How much better to get wisdom than
gold,
to choose understanding rather than
silver!

Success

Malcolm Muggeridge wrote: "When I look back on my life nowadays, which I sometimes do, what strikes me most forcibly about it is that what seemed at that time most significant and seductive, seems now most futile and absurd. For instance, success in all of its various guises; being known and being praised; ostensible pleasures, like acquiring money or seducing women, or traveling, going to and fro in the world and up and down in it like Satan, explaining and experiencing whatever Vanity Fair has to offer. In retrospect, all these exercises in self-gratification seem pure fantasy, what Pascal called, 'licking the earth.'"

Many people work harder and harder climbing the ladder of success only to discover it's leaning against the wrong wall. If the ladder is not leaning against the right wall, every step we take just gets us to the wrong place faster.

True success comes from having God at the center of every aspect of our lives: our family, money, work, possessions, friends, pleasure, and so on. It is not wrong to plan ahead. It is assumed in this passage that we will do so. We may have plans for our job, our family, our church, our holidays, and so on. Whatever our plans, we want them to be a success. Here we see the secret of success. In verse 3 there is a promise and a condition.

1. The condition of success

We are urged, "Commit to the LORD whatever you do" (vs. 3a). What does this mean?

First, it means:

Surrendering our wills

There are two ways to go through life. We can either decide we are perfectly capable of running our own lives. We don't need anyone else—not even God. We make our own plans, without God, to please ourselves. This leads to pride and independence (vs. 5). Alternatively, there is the way of faith. We believe that God wants the very best for our lives (Jeremiah 29:11; Ephesians 2:10). We know that we will not discover His plans until we humbly surrender our wills to Him. That is what it means to become a Christian. We need to stay in that attitude daily, willing to give up any-thing which clashes with His plans.

Secondly, it means to:

Consult with God

This means making all our plans together with God. It may be a help each day to go through our planner committing each event to the Lord. Perhaps at the beginning of each year we might plan ahead with God. God will be concerned about any-thing of concern to us. We need not go to absurd extremes. We don't need to pray about whether to get up in the morning. Certain things are common sense. God does not intend us to be robots—He has given us freedom of choice within the parameters of His Word.

2. The promise of success

The writer says, "Your plans will succeed" (vs. 3b). What does this mean? God is sovereign (vss. 1, 4, 9). "The LORD works out everything for his own ends" (vs. 4). God works within events to bring about His purposes. This does not mean that only good things happen to us but that in and through everything, good and bad, "The LORD works out every-thing for his own ends." Or as St. Paul puts it: "In all things God works for the good of those who love him" (Romans 8:28). There are no loose ends with God. Everything is under His control. Doors may shut and there may be disappointments or doors may open in marvelous ways. Whatever happens, "The LORD determines" your "steps" (vs. 9).

God will work everything out for the good of those who love Him (vss. 6b-7). This does not necessarily mean material prosperity or a life without difficulty (vs. 8) but it does mean a successful life. True success lies in a right relationship with God and a right relationship with other people.

Success can be so dazzling. Many people think they would like a fast car, a big house, loads of money, a touch of fame, and the self-confidence these things *appear* to bring. However, God does not define success in these terms.

Look again at verses 5 and 8. You may want to pray that God would change your understanding of success. Then you will start to experience the thrill and fulfillment of true success: a growing relationship with the God who made us and right relationships with other people.

Prayer:

You might like to begin today by committing to God all your plans for the future—short-term and long-term.

[12]"What do you think? If a man owns a hundred sheep, and one of them wanders away, will he not leave the ninety-nine on the hills and go to look for the one that wandered off? [13]And if he finds it, I tell you the truth, he is happier about that one sheep than about the ninety-nine that did not wander off. [14]In the same way your Father in heaven is not willing that any of these little ones should be lost.

A Brother Who Sins Against You

[15]"If your brother sins against you, go and show him his fault, just between the two of you. If he listens to you, you have won your brother over. [16]But if he will not listen, take one or two others along, so that 'every matter may be established by the testimony of two or three witnesses.' [17]If he refuses to listen to them, tell it to the church; and if he refuses to listen even to the church, treat him as you would a pagan or a tax collector.

[18]"I tell you the truth, whatever you bind on earth will be bound in heaven, and whatever you loose on earth will be loosed in heaven.

[19]"Again, I tell you that if two of you on earth agree about anything you ask for, it will be done for you by my Father in heaven. [20]For where two or three come together in my name, there am I with them."

The Parable of the Unmerciful Servant

[21]Then Peter came to Jesus and asked, "Lord, how many times shall I forgive my brother when he sins against me? Up to seven times?"

[22]Jesus answered, "I tell you, not seven times, but seventy-seven times.

[23]"Therefore, the kingdom of heaven is like a king who wanted to settle accounts with his servants. [24]As he began the settlement, a man who owed him ten thousand talents was brought to him. [25]Since he was not able to pay, the master ordered that he and his wife and his children and all that he had be sold to repay the debt.

[26]"The servant fell on his knees before him. 'Be patient with me,' he begged, 'and I will pay back everything.' [27]The servant's master took pity on him, canceled the debt and let him go.

[28]"But when that servant went out, he found one of his fellow servants who owed him a hundred denarii. He grabbed him and began to choke him. 'Pay back what you owe me!' he demanded.

[29]"His fellow servant fell to his knees and begged him, 'Be patient with me, and I will pay you back.'

[30]"But he refused. Instead, he went off and had the man thrown into prison until he could pay the debt. [31]When the other servants saw what had happened, they were greatly distressed and went and told their master everything that had happened.

[32]"Then the master called the servant in. 'You wicked servant,' he said, 'I canceled all that debt of yours because you begged me to. [33]Shouldn't you have had mercy on your fellow servant just as I had on you?' [34]In anger his master turned him over to the jailers to be tortured, until he should pay back all he owed.

[35]"This is how my heavenly Father will treat each of you unless you forgive your brother from your heart."

Divorce

19 When Jesus had finished saying these things, he left Galilee and went into the region of Judea to the other side of the Jordan. [2]Large crowds followed him, and he healed them there.

Forgiveness

John Plummer was a helicopter pilot during the Vietnam War. He helped organize a napalm raid on the village of Trang Bang in 1972, a bombing immortalized by the prize-winning photograph of one of its victims. In the photo, Phan Thi Kim Phuc, a naked nine-year-old girl, burned, crying, arms outstretched, runs toward the camera with plumes of black smoke billowing in the sky behind her.

For 24 years his conscience tormented him. He badly wanted to find the girl to say that he was sorry. On Veterans' Day, 1996, John met Kim at the Vietnam Memorial. Kim had come to Washington, DC to lay a wreath for peace; John had come with a group of former pilots still searching for freedom from the past. In a speech to the crowd, Kim, now a Christian, said that she forgave the men who had bombed her village. John pushed through the crowds and managed to catch her attention.

He identified himself as the pilot responsible for bombing her village 24 years before, and they were able to talk for two short minutes. "Kim saw my grief, my pain, my sorrow. . . . She held out her arms to me and embraced me. All I could say was "I'm sorry; I'm sorry"—over and over again. And at the same time she was saying, "It's all right, I forgive you."

They met again later the same day, and Kim reaffirmed her forgiveness. They have since become good friends, and call each other regularly. (See The Lost Art of Forgiving, *Johann Christoph Arnold.)*

Forgiveness is never easy but it is vital. We are all human. We make mistakes and we hurt each other. Unforgiveness is at the root of so much quarreling, jealousy, anger, division, slander, gossip, arrogance, and disorder (2 Corinthians 12:20). The teaching of Jesus in this passage is crucial for all relationships: for marriage, family life, church life, relationships at work and in the community and for our eternal destiny. We see three important things about forgiveness.

1. Unlimited forgiveness is commanded by Jesus (vss. 21-22)

The apostle Peter presumably had difficult relationships. He asked Jesus how many times he needed to forgive.

The Jewish teachers taught that we should forgive three times, at most four (on the basis of the book of Amos).

The apostle Peter offers to go further and forgive seven times. He believed in forgiveness. The Jews believed in it. Nearly everybody believes in forgiveness. They would say, "It is right to forgive . . . up to a point. But there comes a point where a person has gone too far and we are justified in not forgiving." The radical part of Jesus' teaching is that He requires unlimited forgiveness.

It does not mean that we condone sin as Christians, nor that there is no place for the law or for justice. The New Testament distinguishes the actions of the state from our responses in personal relationships (see Romans 13). What it does mean is that in our personal relationships we lay aside all malice, revenge, and retribution. Forgiveness is hard, but it is possible.

2. Unlimited forgiveness is a reasonable response to the unlimited forgiveness we have received (vss. 23-30)

A talent was the highest unit of currency, equivalent to 6,000 denarii. The annual revenue from Galilee and Perea was 200 talents. The total revenue of a wealthy province might be 300 talents. 10,000 was the highest Greek numeral, and 10,000 talents was an immense amount, the highest figure imaginable—it was the equivalent for us of "untold millions."

In this story the servant was required to sell his family, not just to repay the debt but also as a form of public humiliation (vs. 25). He pleads for time (vs. 26), which is absurd. He could never pay the debt back. It is the hope of a desperate man. In verse 27 we see in the person of the servant's master what God is like. He does not simply give him time to pay.

He loves him and so is moved to show compassion by canceling the debt and giving the whole family their freedom. He goes way beyond what is required by showing unlimited forgiveness. (We now know that all of this is possible through what Jesus was about to do on the cross.)

Then the forgiven servant finds his fellow servant who owes him 1/600,000 of his debt and aggressively demands payment (vs. 28). In this brilliant short story we side first with the underdog and then are shown the absurdity of a forgiven sinner standing on his rights. Next we find ourselves accusing not the man in the parable but ourselves. The only reasonable response to the unlimited forgiveness of God is unlimited forgiveness of others.

3. Unlimited forgiveness is necessary if we want to be forgiven (vss. 31-35)

The king turns the unforgiving servant over to the jailers "to be tortured." Unforgiveness tortures the soul.

The clear teaching of the New Testament is that we must forgive (Matthew 5:7; Matthew 6:12, 14-15; James 2:13). We do not earn forgiveness. It is made possible through the cross. Our willingness to forgive is evidence that we know God's forgiveness. Once we recognize our need for unlimited forgiveness and have received it, we must forgive others "from the heart," which means totally.

Prayer:

Forgiveness is an act of the will. If there are those whose names come to mind as you read this, choose to forgive them and as an act of the will release them into God's hands. You will probably need to ask for God's help. If you are dealing with very painful issues, it may be wise to seek someone in leadership or a Christian you know and respect to pray with. Ask for God's help to make forgiveness a lifetime habit. We can forgive, not in our own strength but out of the overflow of forgiveness that God has shown us.

Bible Passage
Genesis 3:1-13

²¹So the LORD God caused the man to fall into a deep sleep; and while he was sleeping, he took one of the man's ribs and closed up the place with flesh. ²²Then the LORD God made a woman from the rib he had taken out of the man, and he brought her to the man.

²³The man said,

"This is now bone of my bones
  and flesh of my flesh;
she shall be called 'woman,'
  for she was taken out of man."

²⁴For this reason a man will leave his father and mother and be united to his wife, and they will become one flesh.

²⁵The man and his wife were both naked, and they felt no shame.

The Fall of Man

3 Now the serpent was more crafty than any of the wild animals the LORD God had made. He said to the woman, "Did God really say, 'You must not eat from any tree in the garden'?"

²The woman said to the serpent, "We may eat fruit from the trees in the garden, ³but God did say, 'You must not eat fruit from the tree that is in the middle of the garden, and you must not touch it, or you will die.' "

⁴"You will not surely die," the serpent said to the woman. ⁵"For God knows that when you eat of it your eyes will be opened, and you will be like God, knowing good and evil."

⁶When the woman saw that the fruit of the tree was good for food and pleasing to the eye, and also desirable for gaining wisdom, she took some and ate it. She also gave some to her husband, who was with her, and he ate it. ⁷Then the eyes of both of them were opened, and they realized they were naked; so they sewed fig leaves together and made coverings for themselves.

⁸Then the man and his wife heard the sound of the LORD God as he was walking in the garden in the cool of the day, and they hid from the LORD God among the trees of the garden. ⁹But the LORD God called to the man, "Where are you?"

¹⁰He answered, "I heard you in the garden, and I was afraid because I was naked; so I hid."

¹¹And he said, "Who told you that you were naked? Have you eaten from the tree that I commanded you not to eat from?"

¹²The man said, "The woman you put here with me—she gave me some fruit from the tree, and I ate it."

¹³Then the LORD God said to the woman, "What is this you have done?"

The woman said, "The serpent deceived me, and I ate."

¹⁴So the LORD God said to the serpent, "Because you have done this,

Cursed are you above all the
  livestock
  and all the wild animals!
You will crawl on your belly
  and you will eat dust
  all the days of your life.
¹⁵And I will put enmity
  between you and the woman,
  and between your offspring and
    hers;
he will crush your head,
  and you will strike his heel."

¹⁶To the woman he said,

I will greatly increase your pains in
  childbearing;
  with pain you will give birth to
    children.
Your desire will be for your husband,
  and he will rule over you."

¹⁷To Adam he said, "Because you listened to your wife and ate from the tree about which I commanded you, 'You must not eat of it,'

"Cursed is the ground because of you;
  through painful toil you will eat of it
  all the days of your life.

Loneliness

Loneliness is in essence a home-sickness for God. It is a feeling of not counting, not mattering to anyone, and not being significant. Glenda Jackson said, "It is very lonely being a human being—even when you are in a crowd." Thomas Wolf, the novelist and playwright, said that loneliness is the "central and inevitable fact of human existence." Mother Teresa said, "The greatest disease today is not starvation but loneliness." What is the cause of this loneliness?

Although this passage comes very early in the Bible, we already come across Satan or the devil, seen in this account as a serpent. This image rightly reveals that the devil is both crafty and poisonous. He is real and he is the main opponent of God and of Christian people. Here we see how he tries to change our lives for the worse.

First God gives a wide-ranging **permission:** *"You are free to eat from any tree in the garden" (Genesis 2:16). There is one* **prohibition:** *"but you must not eat from the tree of the knowledge of good and evil" (vs. 17) and God warns of the* **penalty,** *"for when you eat of it you will surely die." In the following verses we see Satan's tactics.*

Step 1—Satan ignores the permission (vs. 1)

Adam and Eve have been given permission by God to eat from any tree in the luscious garden of Eden, except one. Satan ignores the far-reaching and liberal permission.

Step 2—He concentrates on the prohibition (vs. 1)

Satan concentrates on the one prohibition, that they should not eat from the tree of the knowledge of good and evil. Even then he exaggerates, saying that God has banned

the fruit of all the trees (vs. 1). Satan is still the same today. Who do you think upholds the image of Christianity as a restrictive list of rules? He conveniently forgets to portray the enjoyment of knowing Jesus: the peace and freedom, the love and joy.

Step 3—He denies the penalty (vs. 4)

Finally, Satan denies the penalty of disobeying God. By saying, "You will not surely die" (vs. 4), he is suggesting that Adam and Eve will come to no harm if they go against God.

It is a big lie and an effective one. Tragically, our society is living under that lie. It is easy to think that we are missing out on something good if we obey God, but the opposite is true. It is disobedience which causes us to miss out on so much of what God has intended for us, and it is disobedience which ultimately leads us to ruin.

In the verses that follow we see the consequences. They are psychological, theological, and social.

1. Psychological (vs. 7)

Sin affects us by causing an alienation within ourselves. Adam and Eve "sewed fig leaves together and made coverings for themselves." After their sin, they felt shame and embarrassment about being themselves. Having gone astray from God, they were ill at ease within themselves. So often we wear masks to hide our true selves.

2. Theological (vs. 10)

Sin affects our relationship with God as we become alienated from Him. Adam and Eve hid from the Lord God. They were living in God's world without a relationship with Him. That is why loneliness is a home-sickness for God. There is within every human being what is often referred to as "a God-shaped hole."

3. Social (vss. 12-13)

Sin affects our relationships with others and we experience an alienation from our fellow human beings. Adam blamed Eve, Eve blamed the serpent, and the breakdown in human relationships began. We see the continuation of this now in the breakdown of marriages, family life, community life, and on an international scale in war.

Right from the start God is looking to restore the relationship. He calls out, "Where are you?" (vs. 9). There is a hint of the ultimate resolution in verse 15: "he [Jesus] will crush your [Satan's] head, and you [Satan] will strike his [Jesus'] heel." Jesus was nailed to a cross without even a fig leaf to cover him. He was cut off from God and cut off from His friends for us. It is here that we find the answer to our loneliness. As Frank Colquhoun, Anglican author and theologian, said, "When Christ saves a person, He saves them not only from their sin, He also saves them from their solitude."

Once we have entered a relationship with God, our solitude is over. For every person who puts their faith in Christ will one day see Him face to face and be with Him eternally. Even now, by His Spirit, He is always beside us. As you go through the day remember He is with you always.

Prayer:

You might like to pray the prayer of the Psalmist:

Be my shepherd throughout the whole of my life, and when ". . . I walk through the valley of the shadow of death, I will fear no evil, for you are with me" (Psalm 23).

³It is God's will that you should be sanctified: that you should avoid sexual immorality; ⁴that each of you should learn to control his own body in a way that is holy and honorable, ⁵not in passionate lust like the heathen, who do not know God; ⁶and that in this matter no one should wrong his brother or take advantage of him. The Lord will punish men for all such sins, as we have already told you and warned you. ⁷For God did not call us to be impure, but to live a holy life. ⁸Therefore, he who rejects this instruction does not reject man but God, who gives you his Holy Spirit.

⁹Now about brotherly love we do not need to write to you, for you yourselves have been taught by God to love each other. ¹⁰And in fact, you do love all the brothers throughout Macedonia. Yet we urge you, brothers, to do so more and more.

¹¹Make it your ambition to lead a quiet life, to mind your own business and to work with your hands, just as we told you, ¹²so that your daily life may win the respect of outsiders and so that you will not be dependent on anybody.

The Coming of the Lord

¹³Brothers, we do not want you to be ignorant about those who fall asleep, or to grieve like the rest of men, who have no hope. ¹⁴We believe that Jesus died and rose again and so we believe that God will bring with Jesus those who have fallen asleep in him. ¹⁵According to the Lord's own word, we tell you that we who are still alive, who are left till the coming of the Lord, will certainly not precede those who have fallen asleep. ¹⁶For the Lord himself will come down from heaven, with a loud command, with the voice of the archangel and with the trumpet call of God, and the dead in Christ will rise first. ¹⁷After that, we who are still alive and are left will be caught up together with them in the clouds to meet the Lord in the air. And so we will be with the Lord forever. ¹⁸Therefore encourage each other with these words.

5Now, brothers, about times and dates we do not need to write to you, ²for you know very well that the day of the Lord will come like a thief in the night. ³While people are saying, "Peace and safety," destruction will come on them suddenly, as labor pains on a pregnant woman, and they will not escape.

⁴But you, brothers, are not in darkness so that this day should surprise you like a thief. ⁵You are all sons of the light and sons of the day. We do not belong to the night or to the darkness. ⁶So then, let us not be like others, who are asleep, but let us be alert and self-controlled. ⁷For those who sleep, sleep at night, and those who get drunk, get drunk at night. ⁸But since we belong to the day, let us be self-controlled, putting on faith and love as a breastplate, and the hope of salvation as a helmet. ⁹For God did not appoint us to suffer wrath but to receive salvation through our Lord Jesus Christ. ¹⁰He died for us so that, whether we are awake or asleep, we may live together with him. ¹¹Therefore encourage one another and build each other up, just as in fact you are doing.

Final Instructions

¹²Now we ask you, brothers, to respect those who work hard among you, who are over you in the Lord and who admonish you. ¹³Hold them in the highest regard in love because of their work. Live in peace with each other. ¹⁴And we urge you, brothers, warn those who are idle, encourage the timid, help the weak, be patient with everyone. ¹⁵Make sure that nobody pays back wrong for wrong, but always try to be kind to each other and to everyone else.

¹⁶Be joyful always; pray continually;

What Happens When We Die?

The late Canon David Watson who died of cancer at the age of 51 said, "No one can live well until he can die well." Paul wrote this letter to Christian people who were worried about death. They were worried about their relatives and friends who had died and also presumably about themselves. What happens to them and us when we die?

So many people would say that no one knows the answers to these questions, but Paul writes, "We do not want you to be ignorant" (vs. 13). We can find out the answers. Our hope lies in the return of Jesus Christ. There are over 300 references to the second coming in the New Testament. This is not "pie in the sky when you die" but rather the center of our Christian hope, and it is fundamental to our thinking. It involves:

1. A unique hope (vs. 13)

Christians have a unique hope. Paul writes, "We do not want you . . . to grieve like the rest of men, who have no hope" (4:13). It is not wrong to grieve. Grief is important, and we should not suppress it, but the grief of the Christian is (totally) unlike that experienced by those who have no hope. It has been said that "Other people see only a hopeless end, but the Christian rejoices in an endless hope."

2. A certain future (vs. 14)

Hope in the Christian sense is no mere human wishful thinking. It is not a pious hope, theoretical, or speculative. It is not based on emotion, nor is it a crutch. It is built on historical events (vs. 14). Jesus removed the sting of death on the cross as He bore the full horror of death on our behalf. We don't have to face what He has already faced for us. So Paul speaks of death as falling asleep, and falling asleep (if you're anything like me) is something to look forward to. We need not dread death because the next thing we will experience is waking up, and waking up in the presence of God and all who have died in faith. Jesus rose again and demonstrated conclusively that death is conquered. The Resurrection is the guarantee of Christian hope. This total certainty is not arrogant because it is based not on anything we've done or will do but on what Jesus did and said.

3. A glorious eternity (vss. 16-17)

"We will be with the Lord forever," which is the Christian's idea of bliss. There will be no illness, no crying or pain, but only pure joy. This gives a new perspective to this life with all its trials, temptations, and disappointments. We shall never again be parted from the Lord or from those we love. We will be caught up "together with them" (vs. 17). There will be a great reunion in heaven. Paul writes, "Therefore encourage each other with these words" (vs. 18).

4. A sudden judgment (chap. 5:1-3)

Various groups have tried to predict the timing of the Lord's return. But Jesus, Peter, John, and Paul all tell us that He will come back "like a thief in the night" (chap. 5:2). We don't know when this will be. But we do know that He will return. The point is that we must always be ready.

There is a warning in this passage for those who reject Jesus. There is a dark side of our hope. Paul speaks of "destruction" (vs. 3), no escape (vs. 3), and "wrath" (vs. 9). These are solemn and serious words. But he writes to assure the Thessalonians that they have nothing to fear: "But you, brothers, are not in darkness" (5:4). He assures them that they will not "suffer wrath" but will "receive salvation through our Lord Jesus Christ" (vs. 9).

5. A transformed life (chap. 5:4-11)

Not only do we have a unique hope, a certain future, and a glorious eternity, but we are enjoying a foretaste of it now. We are "sons of the light and sons of the day" (ch. 5:5) because God has already broken into history. There is life before death as well as after death: Jesus "died for us so that, whether we are awake or asleep, we may live together with him" (vs. 10).

We are already enjoying the relationship with God which is eternal

"we really feel that the Lord will arrive so— after lunch on Tuesday. —assuming Marjorie's finished her ballet lesson"

life. Yet we cannot simply sit back and enjoy it. If we are aware that others are missing out now and will miss out even more in the future, we must do all we can now to give others hope. As David Watson put it, "Christ wants disciples who not only have hope but also give hope."

Prayer:

Thank God today for the hope He gives us. Thank Him that He has given us all a secure future, that we can look forward to a glorious eternity with the Lord and with all those we love who have died in Christ. Thank Him for rescuing you from the coming judgment. Pray for His help to live a new life, "alert and self-controlled" (vs. 6), "putting on faith and love as a breastplate, and the hope of salvation as a helmet" (vs. 8).

2 Corinthians

1 Paul, an apostle of Christ Jesus by the will of God, and Timothy our brother,

To the church of God in Corinth, together with all the saints throughout Achaia:

²Grace and peace to you from God our Father and the Lord Jesus Christ.

The God of All Comfort

³**Praise be to the God and Father of our Lord Jesus Christ, the Father of compassion and the God of all comfort, ⁴who comforts us in all our troubles, so that we can comfort those in any trouble with the comfort we ourselves have received from God. ⁵For just as the sufferings of Christ flow over into our lives, so also through Christ our comfort overflows. ⁶If we are distressed, it is for your comfort and salvation; if we are comforted, it is for your comfort, which produces in you patient endurance of the same sufferings we suffer. ⁷And our hope for you is firm, because we know that just as you share in our sufferings, so also you share in our comfort.**

⁸**We do not want you to be uninformed, brothers, about the hardships we suffered in the province of Asia. We were under great pressure, far beyond our ability to endure, so that we despaired even of life. ⁹Indeed, in our hearts we felt the sentence of death. But this happened that we might not rely on ourselves but on God, who raises the dead. ¹⁰He has delivered us from such a deadly peril, and he will deliver us. On him we have set our hope that he will continue to deliver us, ¹¹as you help us by your prayers. Then many will give thanks on our behalf for the gracious favor granted us in answer to the prayers of many.**

Paul's Change of Plans

¹²Now this is our boast: Our conscience testifies that we have conducted ourselves in the world, and especially in our relations with you, in the holiness and sincerity that are from God. We have done so not according to worldly wisdom but according to God's grace. ¹³For we do not write you anything you cannot read or understand. And I hope that, ¹⁴as you have understood us in part, you will come to understand fully that you can boast of us just as we will boast of you in the day of the Lord Jesus.

¹⁵Because I was confident of this, I planned to visit you first so that you might benefit twice. ¹⁶I planned to visit you on my way to Macedonia and to come back to you from Macedonia, and then to have you send me on my way to Judea. ¹⁷When I planned this, did I do it lightly? Or do I make my plans in a worldly manner so that in the same breath I say, "Yes, yes" and "No, no"?

¹⁸But as surely as God is faithful, our message to you is not "Yes" and "No." ¹⁹For the Son of God, Jesus Christ, who was preached among you by me and Silas and Timothy, was not "Yes" and "No," but in him it has always been "Yes." ²⁰For no matter how many promises God has made, they are "Yes" in Christ. And so through him the "Amen" is spoken by us to the glory of God.

Going Through Hard Times

We all go through times when things go wrong. We may have experienced hard times: bereavement, rejection, injustice, disappointments, unemployment, financial problems, or relationships going wrong. Why does God allow it? Are there any benefits?

This is the most personal letter Paul wrote. He reveals his feelings as a man of flesh and blood. He knows what it is to be hurt and depressed. He speaks of troubles (vs. 4), sufferings (vss. 5-8), distress (vs. 6), hardships (vs. 8), pressure (vs. 8), despair (vs. 8), sentence of death (vs. 9), and deadly peril (vs. 10).

Paul knew about persecution. He had been imprisoned, chained with three feet of chain to a Roman soldier. He had been flogged five times with 39 lashes. He had been beaten three times with rods. Once he had been stoned. He knew about hardship—lack of sleep, hunger, and thirst. He knew what it was to be cold and naked. He had suffered fatigue and exhaustion. He knew about pressure. He had experienced temptation, sickness, and all the trials of life (2 Corinthians 6:4-10; 11:23-29).

This is not a philosophical or even theological discussion of why God allows suffering. He starts with praise. He is not praising God for the suffering nor seeking it. Instead, in spite of it, he is praising God for the positive benefits which have come out of it. He speaks of seven blessings.

1. The blessing of the presence of God (vs. 4)

The word for comfort (vss. 4-7) means to encourage, cheer, or come alongside. Trouble and persecution can either drive us away from God or closer to Him. God is the "Father of compassion and God of all comfort." As we draw close to Him, we find that He does care and that He suffers with us.

2. The blessing of being able to comfort others (vs. 4)

Those who have suffered themselves are usually the best equipped to help others in their suffering. When we have a tough time, we often become more compassionate and more willing to empathize, support, and help rather than criticize or judge.

3. The blessing of Christian character (vs. 6)

Suffering produces "patient endurance." The Greek word means patience, endurance, fortitude, steadfastness, and perseverance. As gold is refined by fire and as the pruning of the vine produces fruit, so we become purer and more effective as we experience difficulty.

Oscar Wilde wrote, "Now it seems to me that love of some kind is the only possible explanation for the extraordinary amount of suffering that there is in the world . . . because in no other way could the soul of man, for whom the world was made, reach the full stature of its perfection" (*De Profundus,* p. 162).

4. The blessing of Christian friendship (vs. 7)

The Greek word for "share" refers to partnership. We are all partners in Christ, part of the same body. If localized physical pain affects one's whole body, it follows that the suffering of one person in the Body of Christ will bring pain to all. Conversely, the joy of one person will cause all to rejoice. Ultimately, these shared experiences enrich our lives and teach us how to be a true community.

5. The blessing of learning to trust God (vss. 8-9)

When we are in a time of prosperity, we risk becoming independent or proud and may even start to trust ourselves more than God. But, when everything goes wrong and we have reached the end of our own resources there is nothing more we can do. We are thrown into true dependence on God. God's strength is made perfect in weakness (2 Corinthians 12:10).

6. The blessing of seeing God's deliverance (vs. 10)

Paul speaks of the three tenses of God's deliverance: past, present, and future. We are free from the despair of the past, free from any fear of the future, and able to face the present with faith in God.

7. The blessing of answered prayer (vs. 11)

Problems often lead to prayer and prayer often leads to solutions. This in turn leads to God being thanked.

"He has delivered us . . . he will deliver us. On him we have set our hope . . ." (vs. 10). Today, you could thank God for all the ways He has delivered you in the past. Bring to God all the major challenges and problems you face in the weeks and months ahead. Commit them into His hands and set your hope on Him.

"As you help us by your prayers" (vs. 11). Your prayers make a difference. Pray for those you know who are going through hard times at the moment—that "many will give thanks" for the "gracious favor granted . . . in answer to the prayers of many" (vs. 11).

Prayer:

You may like to pray the prayer of Corrie ten Boom:

"Thank You, Lord Jesus that You will be our hiding place, whatever happens."

[16]Therefore do not let anyone judge you by what you eat or drink, or with regard to a religious festival, a New Moon celebration or a Sabbath day. [17]These are a shadow of the things that were to come; the reality, however, is found in Christ. [18]Do not let anyone who delights in false humility and the worship of angels disqualify you for the prize. Such a person goes into great detail about what he has seen, and his unspiritual mind puffs him up with idle notions. [19]He has lost connection with the Head, from whom the whole body, supported and held together by its ligaments and sinews, grows as God causes it to grow.

[20]Since you died with Christ to the basic principles of this world, why, as though you still belonged to it, do you submit to its rules: [21]"Do not handle! Do not taste! Do not touch!"? [22]These are all destined to perish with use, because they are based on human commands and teachings. [23]Such regulations indeed have an appearance of wisdom, with their self-imposed worship, their false humility and their harsh treatment of the body, but they lack any value in restraining sensual indulgence.

Rules for Holy Living

3 Since, then, you have been raised with Christ, set your hearts on things above, where Christ is seated at the right hand of God. [2]Set your minds on things above, not on earthly things. [3]For you died, and your life is now hidden with Christ in God.

[4]When Christ, who is your life, appears, then you also will appear with him in glory.

[5]Put to death, therefore, whatever belongs to your earthly nature: sexual immorality, impurity, lust, evil desires and greed, which is idolatry. [6]Because of these, the wrath of God is coming. [7]You used to walk in these ways, in the life you once lived. [8]But now you must rid yourselves of all such things as these: anger, rage, malice, slander, and filthy language from your lips. [9]Do not lie to each other, since you have taken off your old self with its practices [10]and have put on the new self, which is being renewed in knowledge in the image of its Creator. [11]Here there is no Greek or Jew, circumcised or uncircumcised, barbarian, Scythian, slave or free, but Christ is all, and is in all.

[12]Therefore, as God's chosen people, holy and dearly loved, clothe yourselves with compassion, kindness, humility, gentleness and patience. [13]Bear with each other and forgive whatever grievances you may have against one another. Forgive as the Lord forgave you. [14]And over all these virtues put on love, which binds them all together in perfect unity.

[15]Let the peace of Christ rule in your hearts, since as members of one body you were called to peace. And be thankful. [16]Let the word of Christ dwell in you richly as you teach and admonish one another with all wisdom, and as you sing psalms, hymns and spiritual songs with gratitude in your hearts to God. [17]And whatever you do, whether in word or deed, do it all in the name of the Lord Jesus, giving thanks to God the Father through him.

Rules for Christian Households

[18]Wives, submit to your husbands, as is fitting in the Lord. [19]Husbands, love your wives and do not be harsh with them.

[20]Children, obey your parents in everything, for this pleases the Lord.

[21]Fathers, do not embitter your children, or they will become discouraged.

[22]Slaves, obey your earthly masters in everything; and do it, not only when their eye is on you and to win their favor, but with sincerity of heart and reverence for the Lord. [23]Whatever you do, work at it with all your heart, as working for the Lord, not for men.

A Paradigm Shift

The term "paradigm shift" was introduced by the philosopher of science, Thomas Kuhn. He shows how almost every significant breakthrough in the field of scientific endeavor is first a break with tradition, the old ways of thinking, and the old paradigms. Copernicus created a paradigm shift by seeing the sun, rather than the earth, as the center of the universe. Suddenly everything took on a different interpretation.

The apostle Paul encourages his readers to make a "paradigm shift." A relationship with God through Jesus Christ affects who we are and all our relationships. We should see everything in a new light.

Many of Paul's letters can be divided into two distinct parts. In this one the first part has to do with doctrine (the nature of Christ and the Gospel). The second part is concerned with the practical outworking of becoming a Christian. What we believe affects how we live, which is why what we believe matters so much. Paul writes here that being a Christian will make us different from other people. How does this paradigm shift affect our lives?

1. Change in ourselves (vss. 1-12)

There are many self-help books and much success literature that teach techniques to sort ourselves and our lives out and offer us superficial solutions. But what matters most is much more fundamental: our characters.

We died with Christ, were raised with Him and we will one day appear with Him (vss. 1-4). The old self has died so that we are to get rid of the old ways and live in the power and presence of God. Paul uses an image of changing our clothes: we are to take off old habits and put on new ones.

Take off the old clothes

Firstly, the old clothing may involve the misuse of sex and money (vss. 5-6). There is nothing wrong with these things in themselves except insofar as they are misused and become idols (vs. 5). When this happens, serious consequences follow (vs. 6). Secondly, our old clothing may include sins of speech: using language aggressively and destructively (vss. 8-9).

Thirdly, it may include discrimination (vs. 11). Among Christians there should be no racial, religious, or class barriers. We are all God's chosen people, holy and loved by Him (vs. 12).

We are to put on the new clothes

The new clothes offer us an alternative way of behaving and responding to each other: compassion rather than malice, kindness rather than slander, humility rather than anger, gentleness rather than rage, and patience rather than bad language.

2. Change in our relationships with others (vss. 13-15)

Forgiveness (vs. 13)

Forgiveness is a uniquely Christian virtue. Others may forgive but only Christians have a real basis for it. We have to forgive because we have experienced God's forgiveness. We will never forgive to the extent that we have been forgiven.

Love (vs. 14)

This is not just an emotion but something we are to "put on" and which binds everything else together.

Peace (vs. 15)

The kind of peace that Paul speaks about here is only possible when the peace of Christ is filling our hearts.

3. Change in our attitude to Jesus (vss. 16-17)

Listening to Him (vs. 16a)

We experience a longing to hear Jesus and a thirst for the Word of God. Our priorities change, and we find time to study the Bible regularly, meditating on it and putting it into practice.

Worshiping Him (vs. 16b)

We respond to God's love for us by expressing our love and thankful-ness to Him in worship—"as you sing psalms, hymns and spiritual songs with gratitude in your hearts to God."

Centering our lives on Him (vs. 17)

Whatever we do, whether in word or deed, we should do it all in the name of the Lord Jesus. Our families, our jobs, our friends, money, pos-sessions, and leisure activities are all important and have their place but none of them should be at the center of our lives. That place should be reserved for Jesus and Him alone.

We can change. Jesus died to make it possible for us to live a new life. We must change and as we move on in our life with Jesus, we will change. We will be transformed into His likeness.

Prayer:

O Lord, fill me with the grace of Jesus so that increasingly His beauty may be seen in me.

29"Brothers, I can tell you confidently that the patriarch David died and was buried, and his tomb is here to this day. 30But he was a prophet and knew that God had promised him on oath that he would place one of his descendants on his throne. 31Seeing what was ahead, he spoke of the resurrection of the Christ, that he was not abandoned to the grave, nor did his body see decay. 32God has raised this Jesus to life, and we are all witnesses of the fact. 33Exalted to the right hand of God, he has received from the Father the promised Holy Spirit and has poured out what you now see and hear. 34For David did not ascend to heaven, and yet he said,

" 'The Lord said to my Lord:
　"Sit at my right hand
35until I make your enemies
　a footstool for your feet." '

36"Therefore let all Israel be assured of this: God has made this Jesus, whom you crucified, both Lord and Christ."

37When the people heard this, they were cut to the heart and said to Peter and the other apostles, "Brothers, what shall we do?"

38Peter replied, "Repent and be baptized, every one of you, in the name of Jesus Christ for the forgiveness of your sins. And you will receive the gift of the Holy Spirit. 39The promise is for you and your children and for all who are far off —for all whom the Lord our God will call."

40With many other words he warned them; and he pleaded with them, "Save yourselves from this corrupt generation." 41Those who accepted his message were baptized, and about three thousand were added to their number that day.

The Fellowship of the Believers

42They devoted themselves to the apostles' teaching and to the fellowship, to the breaking of bread and to prayer. 43Everyone was filled with awe, and many wonders and miraculous signs were done by the apostles. 44All the believers were together and had everything in common. 45Selling their possessions and goods, they gave to anyone as he had need. 46Every day they continued to meet together in the temple courts. They broke bread in their homes and ate together with glad and sincere hearts, 47praising God and enjoying the favor of all the people. And the Lord added to their number daily those who were being saved.

Peter Heals the Crippled Beggar

3One day Peter and John were going up to the temple at the time of prayer—at three in the afternoon. 2Now a man crippled from birth was being carried to the temple gate called Beautiful, where he was put every day to beg from those going into the temple courts. 3When he saw Peter and John about to enter, he asked them for money. 4Peter looked straight at him, as did John. Then Peter said, "Look at us!" 5So the man gave them his attention, expecting to get something from them.

6Then Peter said, "Silver or gold I do not have, but what I have I give you. In the name of Jesus Christ of Nazareth, walk." 7Taking him by the right hand, he helped him up, and instantly the man's feet and ankles became strong. 8He jumped to his feet and began to walk. Then he went with them into the temple courts, walking and jumping, and praising God. 9When all the people saw him walking and praising God, 10they recognized him as the same man who used to sit begging at the temple gate called Beautiful, and they were filled with wonder and amazement at what had happened to him.

Where Do I Fit In?

Katherine, a Mennonite woman aged 40, had been sent to a labor farm in Siberia because of her Christian faith. She lived in appalling conditions with no heating, only a board with some straw on it for her bed, and inadequate blankets for warmth.

Her relatives in Canada had for several years tried to get permission from the Russian government for Katherine to come and visit them. Finally permission was granted. When Katherine arrived in Vancouver she couldn't imagine that people could live with so many possessions. She went from relative to relative, staying in their beautiful homes full of beautiful things and was treated royally.

They planned that she should defect, find work, and be cared for by her relatives. But Katherine wanted to go home. She said, "I don't think I can explain to you why it is I want to go back. All I can say is that over here in this country, you people have your things and you are busy all day long. Over there we don't have anything, but we have each other. I want to get back to my brothers and sisters in Christ where we live for one another."

These verses in Acts describe the church just after it had swelled to over 3,000 people in its first day of existence! Exciting things happen when the people of God get together to celebrate. We see that in the great festivals of the Old Testament and we see it again around the world today. At this festival of Pentecost people had experienced the visible and audible presence of God (Acts 2:1-4). There must have been an incredible sense of worship and awe. But awe-inspiring times of celebration where hundreds or thousands of people gather to worship may simultaneously inspire us and make us feel lonely.

Such experiences may lead us to ask: "Where do I fit it?" "How can I make friends?" "How can I contribute?" "How can I grow in my faith?" "How can I be more effective?" or "What can I do?" The answers were found in the groups of Christians which gathered in homes after Pentecost. They were led by ordinary people (Acts 18:1-3; Romans 16:3-5; 1 Corinthians 16:19), men and women doing ordinary jobs. Similar groups exist today, and are at the heart of church life.

On the day of Pentecost the disciples had experienced the love of God being poured into their hearts by the Holy Spirit (Romans 5:5). Now this love overflowed in three directions.

1. They loved God

Teaching (vs. 42a)

"They devoted themselves to the apostles' teaching."

They wanted to know what God was saying to them. This "teaching" can now be found in the New Testament. Through the Bible, God speaks to us and we get to know Jesus Christ better. Home groups are an ideal place to study the Bible together.

Prayer (vs. 42b)

Their prayer meetings were never dull. They were times of great excitement. Again, home groups are the ideal place to pray for one another, especially if we are going through difficult times. We can also unite in small groups to pray for specific issues, individuals, or for our country.

Food (vs. 42)

They had a meal together and in the "breaking of bread" they remembered Jesus' presence and death for them.

Worship (vs. 47)

They praised God together. We should expect to meet God intimately through worship. This is the highest and most fulfilling calling that we can know. Our main purpose in life is "to glorify God and enjoy Him forever" (Westminster Catechism).

2. They loved one another

Eric Fromm writes in his book *The Sane Society,* "There is not much love to be found in the world of our day. There is rather a superficial friendliness concealing a distance, an indifference, a subtle distrust." In a world characterized by loneliness, alienation, and individualism, there is a greater need than ever to belong. The church of Jesus Christ and in particular the small group is the place to find Christian friendship and fellowship.

Home groups are places to love and be loved, to encourage, and be encouraged. The atmosphere should be open, non-judgmental, and honest enough to allow friendships to deepen (see Romans 16:3-4). It should be a group of people who stick with one another through thick and thin. We should know we can rely on one another and trust each other totally.

They demonstrated love

These early Christians did not just feel love but they loved one another practically and actively on a daily basis. It has been said that if Christians were for one day what they ought to be, the world would be converted overnight.

They supported one another

There was a radical generosity of spirit which was entirely voluntary (Acts 4:34). They renounced possessiveness and shared their resources. Generosity takes many forms: giving financially to one another, sharing our possessions, and making time for one another, offering hospitality and practical help.

They used their gifts

Each person contributed their gifts: teaching, hospitality, giving, or leading worship. The small group is the place where we discover where we fit in. We minister to one another as parts of the body of Christ and find that our different gifts complement each other.

They had fun together

They "ate together with glad and sincere hearts" (vs. 46). A gloomy Christian is a contradiction in terms. A home group should be, among other things, a place of laughter and enjoyment.

3. They loved the world

They went out into the world with wonders and miraculous signs (vs. 43). They were respected by everyone and the Lord added to their number (vs. 47). They looked outward. If small groups look inward they will stagnate and die. If they are looking out they will have the joy of seeing other people's lives changed, the same sort of joy that parents have watching their children growing up.

The small group is not always easy because all of us can be difficult to help and difficult to love. However, we are changed by shared experience, and within the highs and lows of such a group, we discover the joy of true relationship (e.g., see Apollos—Acts 18:24; 1 Corinthians 1:12; 3:4-6; 4:6; Titus 3:13).

This is the church when it's most vibrant and attractive. It is vital to be an active participant in a church which encourages you in your faith and gives you an opportunity to serve God. We cannot do it on our own.

Prayer:

If you do not already belong to such a group, pray that God will guide you and then seek out such a gathering.

²⁶He lifts up a banner for the distant
  nations,
  he whistles for those at the ends of
  the earth.
Here they come,
  swiftly and speedily!
²⁷Not one of them grows tired or
  stumbles,
  not one slumbers or sleeps;
not a belt is loosened at the waist,
  not a sandal thong is broken.
²⁸Their arrows are sharp,
  all their bows are strung;
their horses' hoofs seem like flint,
  their chariot wheels like a whirlwind.
²⁹Their roar is like that of the lion,
  they roar like young lions;
they growl as they seize their prey
  and carry it off with no one to
  rescue.
³⁰In that day they will roar over it
  like the roaring of the sea.
And if one looks at the land,
  he will see darkness and distress;
  even the light will be darkened by
  the clouds.

Isaiah's Commission

6In the year that King Uzziah died, I
saw the Lord seated on a throne,
high and exalted, and the train of his
robe filled the temple. ²Above him were
seraphs, each with six wings: With two
wings they covered their faces, with two
they covered their feet, and with two
they were flying. ³And they were calling
to one another:

  Holy, holy, holy is the LORD
    Almighty;
  the whole earth is full of his
    glory."

⁴At the sound of their voices the
doorposts and thresholds shook and
the temple was filled with smoke.
⁵"Woe to me!" I cried. "I am ruined!
For I am a man of unclean lips, and I
live among a people of unclean lips, and

my eyes have seen the King, the LORD
Almighty."
⁶Then one of the seraphs flew to me
with a live coal in his hand, which he
had taken with tongs from the altar.
⁷With it he touched my mouth and said,
"See, this has touched your lips; your
guilt is taken away and your sin atoned
for."
⁸Then I heard the voice of the Lord
saying, "Whom shall I send? And who
will go for us?"
  And I said, "Here am I. Send me!"

⁹He said, "Go and tell this people:

  " 'Be ever hearing, but never
    understanding;
  be ever seeing, but never
    perceiving.'
¹⁰Make the heart of this people
    calloused;
  make their ears dull
  and close their eyes.
Otherwise they might see with their
    eyes,
  hear with their ears,
  understand with their hearts,
and turn and be healed."

¹¹Then I said, "For how long, O Lord?"
And he answered:

"Until the cities lie ruined
  and without inhabitant,
until the houses are left deserted
  and the fields ruined and ravaged,
¹²until the LORD has sent everyone far
    away
  and the land is utterly forsaken.
¹³And though a tenth remains in the
    land,
  it will again be laid waste.
But as the terebinth and oak
  leave stumps when they are cut
    down,
  so the holy seed will be the stump in
    the land."

How My Life Was Changed

There is great power in a testimony. In this passage the prophet Isaiah speaks about how God turned his life around in about 736 B.C. God revealed to him what was going on around him, and Isaiah describes the state of affairs in Israel in the first five chapters of the book of Isaiah. The people had turned their backs on God (1:4). There was corruption (1:4), formality in religion (1:11), materialism, arrogance, godlessness, drunkenness, and carousing (5:20-27). God called him to do something about it by speaking out to his generation. How did this happen?

1. He caught a glimpse of who God really is (vss. 1-4)

Isaiah tries to describe what he has seen of the majesty, holiness, glory, and power of God in language which we may find difficult to relate to. He is using his own words to describe a powerful encounter with the living God.

2. He felt totally unworthy and inadequate for the task (vs. 5)

When he saw the holiness of God he said, "Woe to me! I am ruined!" Our sense of sin is related to how close we are to God. The closer we are to the light the more we are aware of the dirt. First, he is aware of his own sin. He says, "I am a man of unclean lips." Secondly, he realizes that he lives among a people of unclean lips, surrounded by sin. We pick up dirt as we walk through the world. We cannot avoid it.

Isaiah has a sense of his own unworthiness and inadequacy. God breaks our hearts as He shows us what we are like. Oscar Wilde wrote: "A man's very highest moment is, I have no doubt at all, when he kneels in the dust, and beats his breast, and tells all the sins of his life" (*De Profundus* p. 197).

But God does not leave us there . . .

3. He experiences the mercy of God (vs. 6)

Our guilt would destroy us but God took the initiative and provided the means of our cleansing. He took away Isaiah's guilt and atoned for his sin. Now we understand that this was possible through the cross of Jesus Christ. We all have the opportunity to experience His forgiveness and His love. In spite of all we have done, God loves us.

The experience of our own sin is the answer to pride. The experience of the love of God is the answer to insecurity. Both were dealt with at the cross. Without Him we can do nothing (John 15:5). "I can do everything through him . . ." (Philippians 4:13).

The past is dealt with. We do not need to go around loaded with guilt but rather filled with the knowledge of God's love for us.

4. He responded to God's call (vs. 8)

God asked him the question: "I have done all this for you—now will you go for me?" His whole life was before him. What was he going to do with it? His response was to surrender his will. He said, "Here am I. Send me!" (vs. 8). He did not make any excuses. He didn't say, "I am too busy." He didn't offer to do it later, or when he was less tired or had sorted out some problem.

It was an unconditional response. He didn't say, "Send me, I am going that way anyhow" or "Send me, I was planning to do that" or "Send me, I rather like the sound of that idea." He said, "Send me to do anything you want, Lord." That is true commitment and true service. Isaiah gave God a straight "yes." We need to do the same. We will never have a better opportunity than now.

Isaiah was willing to be used as a servant and God sent him to speak to the entire nation. When we say to God, "Here I am. Send me!" He will use us as His servant. This may well be in our place of work, with our family, or with our neighbors and friends. In due course, it may even be further afield. In that case He will give us clear guidance.

We, unlike Isaiah, are living in the age of the Spirit when the Holy Spirit has come to live in every Christian. If God wanted to do this for Isaiah, how much more will He do it for you?

Prayer:

Have you caught a glimpse of God? Ask God to reveal Himself to you: His majesty, holiness, glory, and power. When we catch a glimpse of God, we feel compelled to confess our own unworthiness and ask Him for His mercy. Then we can offer ourselves to His service by saying, "Here I am. Send me."

Alpha

This book is an Alpha resource. The Alpha course is a practical introduction to the Christian faith initiated by Holy Trinity Brompton church in London, and now being run by thousands of churches throughout the U.K. and around the world.

For more information on Alpha, including details of tapes, videos, and training manuals, contact the following.

Alpha U.S.A.
2275 Half Day Road
Suite 185
Deerfield, IL 60015
Tel: 800.362.5742
Tel: + 212.406.5269
e-mail: info@alphausa.org
www.alphausa.org

Alpha in the Caribbean
Holy Trinity Brompton
Brompton Road
London SW7 1JA UK
Tel: +44 (0) 845.644.7544
e-mail: americas@alpha.org
www.alpha.org

Alpha Canada
Suite #230 – 11331 Coppersmith Way
Riverside Business Park
Richmond, BC V7A 5J9
Tel: 800.743.0899
Fax: 604.271.6124
e-mail: office@alphacanada.org
www.alphacanada.org

To purchase resources in Canada:

David C. Cook Distribution Canada
P.O. Box 98, 55 Woodslee Avenue
Paris, ON N3L 3E5
Tel: 800.263.2664
Fax: 800.461.8575
e-mail: custserve@davidccook.ca
www.davidccook.ca

Alpha Titles Available

Why Jesus?
A booklet given to all participants at the start of the Alpha course.

"The clearest, best illustrated, and most challenging short presentation of Jesus that I know." Michael Green

Why Christmas?
The Christmas version of *Why Jesus?*

Why Easter?
The Easter version of *Why Jesus?*

Questions of Life
The Alpha course in book form, providing a practical introduction to the Christian faith. Each chapter addresses basic and foundational questions, while pointing the way to an authentic Christianity, relevant to today's world.

Telling Others
The Alpha conference presented in book form. *Telling Others* imparts the vision, excitement and challenge of Alpha and is the resource for churches and individuals that wish to run this course within their communities.

Searching Issues
The seven issues most often raised by participants in the Alpha course: suffering, other religions, sex before marriage, the New Age, homosexuality, science and Christianity, and the Trinity.

A Life Worth Living
Nine talks based on the Book of Philippians. This is an invaluable next step for those who have completed the Alpha course, and for anyone eager to put their faith on a firm biblical footing.

The Jesus Lifestyle
An in-depth look at the Sermon on the Mount (Matthew 5–7), showing that Jesus' teaching flies in the face of modern lifestyle and presents us with a radical alternative.

All titles are by Nicky Gumbel, who is the Vicar of Holy Trinity Brompton church in London.